D0006704

Euclid Public Library
631 E. 222nd Street
Euclid, Ohio 44123

A
JANE
AUSTEN
CHRISTMAS

*Celebrating the Season
of Romance, Ribbons & Mistletoe*

BY CARLO DEVITO

CIDER MILL PRESS

BOOK
PUBLISHERS

A Jane Austen Christmas
Copyright © 2015 Carlo DeVito

This is an officially licensed edition by Cider Mill Press Book Publishers LLC
All rights reserved under the Pan-American and International Copyright Conventions.

No part of this book may be reproduced in whole or in part, scanned, photocopied, recorded,
distributed in any printed or electronic form, or reproduced in any manner whatsoever, or
by any information storage and retrieval system now known or hereafter invented, without
express written permission of the publisher, except in the case of brief quotations embodied in
critical articles and reviews.

The scanning, uploading, and distribution of this book via the Internet or via any
other means without permission of the publisher is illegal and punishable by law.
Please support authors' rights, and do not participate in or encourage
piracy of copyrighted materials.

13 Digit ISBN: 978-1-60433-591-0
10 Digit ISBN: 1-60433-591-2

This book may be ordered by mail from the publisher.
Please include $4.95 for postage and handling.
Please support your local bookseller first!

Books published by Cider Mill Press Book Publishers are available at special discounts for bulk
purchases in the United States by corporations, institutions, and other organizations. For more
information, please contact the publisher.

Cider Mill Press Book Publishers
"Where good books are ready for press"
12 Spring Street | P.O. Box 454
Kennebunkport, Maine 04046
Visit us on the web! www.cidermillpress.com

Cover design by Whitney Cookman & Shelby Newsted
Interior design by Shelby Newsted
Typography: Nuptial Script, Vendome, Goudy Old Style, Copperplate Gothic

Image Credits:
Decorative headers and borders, Seamartini Graphics/Shutterstock.com; decorative frame,
100ker/Shutterstock.com; endpapers, Rodina Olena/Shutterstock.com; pp. 27-28, Park's
Shakespeare characters, courtesy Folger Shakespeare Library; p. 32, courtesy Gutenberg Project;
p. 52, antique wooden lap desk, courtesy Wikimedia Commons/Koppas; p. 69, courtesy Historic
Odessa Foundation of Delaware; pp. 74-75, caricature of longways dance by Rowlandson (1790s),
courtesy Wikimedia Commons; p. 82, miniature portrait by George Englehart; p. 103, *Dictionary
of the Vulgar Tongue* by Francis Grose (1785); p. 124, Jane Austen's house, Chawton, courtesy
Wikimedia Commons/Rudi Riet; p. 145, Martha Lloyd's recipe book, courtesy Jane Austen's
House Museum; p. 149, nicoolay/iStock.com; p. 157, Archimboldus/Shutterstock.com

℗ Public domain images via Wikimedia Commons: 11, 14, 17, 18, 20,
49, 52, 57, 74-75, 93, 94, 106, 110, 122, 124, 127, 163, 177

Printed in the United States of America

1 2 3 4 5 6 7 8 9 0
First Edition

This book is dedicated to my sisters,
Claudia Pazmany and Leigh Ann DeVito.
Many Happy Christmas returns!

This little bag I hope will prove

To be not vainly made—

For, if you should a needle want

It will afford you aid.

And as we are about to part

T'will serve another end,

For when you look upon the Bag

You'll recollect your friend

—A note by Jane Austen, attached to a needlework bag
given as a gift to a departing friend, January 1792

Contents

INTRODUCTION

Who wouldn't want to have a Jane Austen Christmas? Austen mentions Christmas in each of her six main novels, and most have vividly described scenes set during the holiday season. Mr. Elton's tipsy Christmas Eve proposal to Emma Woodhouse; Anne Elliot's holiday call on the Musgroves at Uppercross, with the brightly burning Yule log and girls cutting up silk and gold paper; the newly engaged Elizabeth Bennet inviting her aunt Gardiner to Pemberley for Christmas—Janeites recall these scenes with delight, perhaps even during their own holiday celebrations.

Many of the traditions associated with what we think of as a typical English Christmas are from the Victorian era, several decades after Jane Austen's books were published. There are no Christmas trees in Austen's scenes, no extravagant gift-giving, no sentimental spirit of the holiday. Jane Austen's novels do not lend themselves to feel-good holiday movie adaptations. However, the Christmas-related scenes and mentions all have to do with visiting family and friends, extending hospitality, and the gathering together of loved ones. Through Jane Austen's letters, we know that Austen treasured time with her family above all else; though the family had their little traditions, companionship was all that was needed to produce holiday cheer.

Austen was writing for an audience of her own contemporaries. She did not have to describe the minute details of holiday celebrations among the British gentry because those reading her books would already know them. Thus, the 21st-century Janeite who wishes to incorporate these traditions into her own winter holidays might have some difficulty pinpointing the details. How should one decorate? What should one serve at a celebratory dinner? What happens on which day? These are questions that can only be answered by digging deeper.

In this book, Carlo DeVito has done what Jane Austen didn't need to do: describe the details of a typical British Christmas in the late Georgian era in which Austen's books take place. Drawing on Austen family letters and memoirs, he has described the "Christmas gaieties" in which Austen herself would have taken part—everything from amateur theatricals to religious observances to a delightfully messy game of bullet pudding. (What's that? Keep reading, and you'll soon find out.) There is plenty of period detail, including recipes for holiday delicacies, rules for card and other games played at Christmas parties, and explanations of the intricacies of dancing at a ball.

But this book is not just an enumeration of the dances, games, and meals of a Georgian Christmas. It is a timeline of Christmases celebrated by Jane Austen during her life, during which she experienced the joy of first love, the sorrow of loss, and the triumph of successful publication. All of these experiences colored her work and gave it depth and nuance. Austen was not a stenographer who simply transferred real-life experiences to her novels; she was an artist, who spiced her creations with the emotions we all share as human beings. Austen's family experienced love and loss as well—including the loss of Jane herself. Like Austen's works, her memory lived on for her sister Cassandra, her brothers, and her nieces and nephews, and lives today in the hearts and minds of her devoted fans, at Christmas and all year long.

So go forth, good Janeite, and learn what it takes to make a Jane Austen Christmas. Light the Yule log, dance down a long set, enjoy some mince pie and punch, and revel in the warmth and light of the season, Jane Austen-style.

—Margaret C. Sullivan,
author of *The Jane Austen Handbook*

Portrait of Jane Austen
by James Andrews, c. 1870

1786

PART ONE: 1786

The year was 1786, and a raucous gang of boys were running around the grounds of the roomy brick home, with its wavy-glassed windows and several shadowy gables. Playfully pushing each other around, one or two of the jubilant boys might have ripped their britches before making their way up the broad steps of the manse for the last time that year. Their bags packed, one by one, they waved goodbye to the Steventon Rectory. They loudly proclaimed the holiday and wished one another and the Austen family well.

The school at the Steventon Rectory was overseen by George Austen, Jane Austen's father. Born in 1731, George's mother died in childbirth and his father passed a year after marrying a new wife, who, newly widowed, did

Engraving of Steventon Rectory, Hampshire, 1871

not want the responsibility of taking care of the young lad. "George then lived with an aunt in Tonbridge and earned a Fellowship to study at St. John's. Smart, ambitious, and self-made (with the support of his uncle Francis), he received a Bachelor of Arts, a Master of Arts, and a Bachelor of Divinity degree at Oxford. Considered good looking all his life, he was called 'the handsome proctor' as he worked as an assistant chaplain, dean of arts, and Greek lecturer while going to school," wrote Victorian Sanborn, a lifetime member of the Jane Austen Society of North America.

Anna LeFroy, Jane's niece, described the Reverend George Austen as "extremely handsome, and it was a beauty which stood by him all his life. At the time when I have the most perfect recollection of him he must have been hard upon seventy, but his hair in its milk-whiteness might have belonged to a much older man. It was very beautiful, with short curls about the ears. His eyes were not large, but of a peculiar and bright hazel. My aunt Jane's were something like them, but none of the children had precisely the same excepting my uncle Henry."

George Austen married Cassandra Leigh in 1764 and settled with his family in the modest village of Steventon. According to local historian Audrey Hawkridge, Steventon "lies nestled in a quiet spot between two main routes from Basingstoke: the Andover road at Deane to the north, where stage coaches to and from London halted twice a day, and the Winchester road to the south near Dummer, which was known as Popham Lane. The late 17th century house, repaired in the 1760s for the Austens' occupation, had seven bedrooms. Its flat facade was broken up by evenly placed windows, and a trellised porch almost more suited to a cottage formed a centrepiece."

The Steventon parsonage was "situated low and subject to be flooded, distant from the greater part of the village and in a dilapidated state," according to the Knight Family Papers, Hampshire Record Office, Winchester.

Cassandra kept a kitchen garden, and George farmed the estate to supply food for their ever-growing family.

"Outside there were fields where Mr. Austen farmed and his wife grew potatoes (at that time quite an innovation), formal gardens with a turf walk, a sundial, strawberry beds, and a grassy bank down which the young Jane possibly enjoyed rolling as a child," continued Hawkridge. "There was also a carriage sweep, and a barn used for private theatricals except in winter, when the dining room had to suffice. Later, a double hedgerow with mixed shrubs and wildflowers was added, for use as a private footpath to the church. At the side of the Rectory were chestnut, fir and elm trees."

According to Sanborn, "[Mr. Austen's] annual income from the combined tithes of Steventon and the neighboring village of Deane was modest. With so many mouths to feed, the family was not wealthy."

"They certainly weren't well off. They . . . were very much part of the village life. It was a working house and they took care of themselves. You get the impression they were a hard-working family—they were into the good life," said project director Debbie Charlton of Archaeo Briton, who recently headed up an archeological dig of Austen's childhood home.

As famed literary historian and Austen biographer Claire Tomalin wrote, "A village rector in a remote country parish

St. Nicholas Church, Steventon, Hampshire

was as much a real farmer as a shepherd of souls." Reverend and farmer Mr. Austen not only shepherded his young parishioners into church but also advised them academically.

"To augment the family income, George Austen opened a boarding school at Steventon Rectory for the sons of local gentlemen," wrote Sanborn. This, combined with the income and food from the farm, proved enough for the Austen family.

At the beginning of December as Christmastide approached, the boys who had attended school throughout the fall would leave Steventon for home, allowing the Austen family to spend time together and entertain visiting relatives from nearby towns.

Cassandra Austen

Young Jane Austen was one of eight children born to George and Cassandra. They both came from country gentry and enjoyed a modest but genteel enough life. She had six bothers and one sister, Cassandra, who was two years older than she, and who would become her best friend and confidant for the rest of her life.

The Austen family very much looked forward to Christmastide. With the release of his charges for the holidays, Reverend Austen and his family would expect to see the return of their own sons, who were away at boarding school, for the season. Austen was acutely aware of this, for their return was a highlight of the year for young Jane and Cassandra.

"Washington Irving, in his Sketch Book of Geoffrey Crayon, Gentleman, also records the return home of the schoolboys as a major feature of Christmas at this time," wrote historical romance writer Jo Beverley.

Austen relayed a scene in Chapter 14 of *Persuasion* that surely would have mimicked a similar scene at Steventon Rectory:

> *Immediately surrounding Mrs. Musgrave were the little Harvilles, whom she was sedulously guarding from the tyranny of the two children from the Cottage, expressly arrived to amuse them. On one side was a table occupied by some chattering girls, cutting up silk and gold paper; and on the other were trestles and trays, bending under the weight of brawn and cold pies, where riotous boys were holding high revel; the whole completed by a roaring Christmas fire, which seemed determined to be heard in spite of the noise of the others.*

But this Christmastide was not just memorable for the reuniting of their immediate family. Jane Austen's inspiration and her career would be catapulted right from this very singular, very magical Christmas season.

Eliza de Feuillide

"The Christmas holiday of 1786 promised a lot of excitement: Phila Hancock and her daughter were about to reappear on the scene for the first time since they had gone to live in France in 1777," wrote Austen expert Jon Spence. Philadelphia Hancock was George Austen's sister and a favorite with Jane and Cassy. She was proposed to be the inspiration for a number of characters in Jane's works.

Phila's daughter was named Eliza de Feuillide. Fourteen years Jane's senior, Eliza was born in India and had married a French Army Captain, Jean-François Capot de Feuillide, a self-styled count. She was pregnant when she was on the way to visit the Austens and had every intention of having the baby in England, but instead gave birth in Calais.

"I mean," Eliza wrote, "to spend a very few days in London, and, if my health allows me, immediately to pay a visit to Steventon, because my uncle informs us that Midsummer and Christmas are the only seasons when his mansion is sufficiently at liberty to admit of his receiving his friends."

Now, with Jane and Cassy older, and their brothers returning, the family regained its cohesion as they prepared to spend the season together.

———————

Christmastide was of course all the more special for Jane, as her birthday was December 16th. In the year of her birth, Jane was christened at home by her father, with a formal church ceremony that followed. Reverend Austen wrote that he and his wife were pleased at the idea of having a second daughter, "a present plaything for her sister Cassy and a future companion. She is to be Jenny."

"Inside the parsonage, Mrs. Austen lay upstairs in the four-poster, warmly bundled under her feather-beds, the baby in her cradle beside her," wrote Tomalin. "Mrs. Austen would not be expected to set foot on the floor for at least two weeks."

Because of the snowy conditions of the season and the remoteness of the region, Tomalin wrote, "Neighbors could not easily call, except for a few robust gentlemen on horseback, bringing congratulatory messages and gifts from their wives. On Christmas eve the children laid out the traditional holly branches on the window ledges, and on Christmas morning Mr. Austen, well booted and coated, set off up the hill to his tiny, unheated stone church, St. Nicholas, hoping the light would suffice to read the lesson and serve the sacrament to those farmers and villagers who turned out to hear him." After services, Mr. Austen would return home, "back down the hill, through the snow and silence. There were not more than thirty families living in Steventon, the single row of cottages at some distance from the parsonage; and there was neither shop nor inn."

Christmas up to the time of Janes Austen's life had borne several unsavory periods in English history.

Before the Puritans came to power, Christmas had become a raucous holiday, famed for wassailing, caroling, and general mischief. Wassailing was a custom that had dated back to pre-Norman conquest England, in which apple growers sang songs to scare away evil spirits and wake up the tress during the dead of winter. Generally a communal time of rejoicing and preparation, wassailing during the Christmas season was slightly different. The idea was to knock on neighbors' doors, and they would welcome the visitors, offering warm punch and food. In the best of circumstances, it was a roaming party of good cheer that would trip through the neighborhoods greeting each one another.

"In England in the Middle Ages, this period was one of continuous feasting and merrymaking, which climaxed on Twelfth Night, the traditional end of the Christmas season. In Tudor England, Twelfth Night itself was forever solidified in popular culture when William Shakespeare used it as the setting for one of his most famous stage plays, titled *Twelfth Night*. Often a Lord of Misrule was chosen to lead the Christmas revels," wrote journalist Walter Brooks. "Some of these traditions were adapted from the older pagan customs, including the Roman Saturnalia and the Germanic Yuletide."

By the mid-1600s wassailing became associated with rowdy bands of young men who would enter the homes of wealthy neighbors, demanding free food and drink, as was the custom. If the householder refused, the master and mistress were usually cursed, and in some cases the houses were vandalized. The old carol, "We Wish You a Merry Christmas," usually considered a hailing of good will, could be reinterpreted as a demand for "figgy pudding" and "good cheer" (aka the wassail bowl and beverage), without which the wassailers in the song refuse to leave, saying "We won't go until we get some, so bring some out here." Today's popular Christmas carol belies the more sinister tone many surely experienced.

According to J. F. Wakefield of Austenonly.com, "Christmas was a vibrant celebration in England until the Interregnum or the period of the Commonwealth in the mid-17th century, when Charles I had been deposed and beheaded and England was governed by Puritans."

In the centuries prior to the Georgian kings, Christmas in England became a dismal affair. In 1644 the holiday was banned by Oliver Cromwell, who called it "an extreme forgetfulness of Christ, by giving liberty to carnal and sensual delights," wrote Laura Boyle, proprietor of Austenation: Regency Accessories.

According to Wakefield, "The Puritans disliked Christmas because of its Popish and heathenish history, and most of all because of its associations with consumption of extravagant food, drink, dancing, and theatrical productions . . . Puritans also believed there was no scriptural justification for the celebration of Christmas, as nowhere in the Bible does it mention that the Nativity of Christ should be observed as a festival. They saw no factual or scriptural basis for Christ's birth date being designated as the 25th December. They believed that Christmas was nothing more than a pragmatic festival created by the early Catholic Church as a means of incorporating, and thereby making holy, the pagan winter solstice celebrations . . . Between 1644 and 1647 the Commonwealth Parliament introduced a series of measures all designed to curb the excesses of the populace during the Christmas season."

"Carols were forbidden; anyone caught cooking a goose or baking a Christmas cake or boiling a pudding was in danger of fine, confiscation or worse," wrote Boyle.

Eventually, the monarchy in England was restored, but Christmas remained somewhat subdued.

Jane and Cassandra lived during the Georgian period, 1714 to 1830, which took its name from the reign of the first four Hanoverian kings of Great Britain: George I, George II, George III and George IV. The Regency period, which was so strongly identified with Jane (because most of her published works became well known within that period), occupied the years of 1811 to 1820, during the Regency of George IV as Prince of Wales during the illness of his father George III, and the last years of Jane's life.

Most of Jane's adult life coincided with the overlapping Napoleonic Period from 1803 to 1815. The fashion and the tastes of the First French Empire greatly influenced art, fashion, and architecture, among many things.

"The period of Napoleonic rule lends its name to the late Neoclassical style that characterizes artistic creations of the era, including the Directory and Consulate periods," wrote Metropolitan Museum of Art's Cybele Gontar. "Courts across Europe adopted the Empire style, especially in Russia, where it became a staple. In Germany and Austria, it coexisted with the gentler Biedermeier associated with modest domestic interiors." In the later half of Jane's life, the Regency style became all the rage in England, and a rival to the Empire, both stylistically and politically. So, not only were France and England's armies at war, but their trend setters were as well.

Christmas in Jane's day worked off of a different calendar. In Jane and Cassandra's time, the official season began early, on December 6th, St. Nicholas Day, when many people would start a round of holiday visits. City dwellers would usually go to their friends' or family's country estates. Gentry who already lived in more agricultural areas would visit one another, sometimes for extended periods. This series of visits would usually last through the beginning of January, generally speaking, ending sometime after Twelfth Night.

"Twelfth Night is a festival, in some branches of Christianity marking the coming of the Epiphany," explains journalist Martin Beckford. "Different traditions mark the date of Twelfth Night on either 5th January or 6th January; the Church of England, Mother Church of the Anglican Communion, celebrates Twelfth Night on the 5th and refers to the night before Epiphany, the day when the nativity story tells us that the three wise men visited the infant Jesus." For the Austens, the Western Church traditions meant that

Envelope for Shakespeare Character Sheet by A. Park, c. 1830, Folger Shakespeare Library

the Twelfth Night concluded the Twelve Days of Christmas, although for some the Twelfth Night may have preceded the Twelfth Day.

"We know, from reading Jane Austen's letters, that she, along with the rest of Georgian England, celebrated Twelfth Night, the culmination of twelve days of celebrating, beginning Christmas Day. Twelfth Night, which marked the official end of the festivities, was a highly anticipated holiday which included games (such as Charades and Tableau Vivants) and

Shakespeare Character Sheet by A. Park, c. 1840, Folger Shakespeare Library

special foods, like Twelfth Night Cake," wrote Boyle. "The
time leading up to this celebration was, of course, called The

Twelve Days of Christmas, and as the song of the same name implies, it was a time for true lovers to meet, fall in love, or even marry. The twelve days after Christmas were often the scene for house parties and balls . . . "

Christmas historian Bruce Forbes wrote, "In 567 the Council of Tours proclaimed that the entire period between Christmas and Epiphany should be considered part of the celebration, creating what became known as The Twelve Days of Christmas, or what the English called Christmastide. On the last of the twelve days, called Twelfth Night, various cultures developed a wide range of additional special festivities. The variation extends even to the issue of how to count the days. If Christmas Day is the first of the twelve days, then Twelfth Night would be on January 5th, the eve of Epiphany. If December 26th, the day after Christmas, is the first day, then Twelfth Night falls on January 6th, the evening of Epiphany itself."

As the parishioner boys departed Reverend Austen's school, Jane and Cassandra might have embarked on decorating the Steventon Rectory for Christmastide. Jane and Cassandra, for example, might have gone out and collected cuttings from various trees and shrubs in and around the country lanes of Steventon. They would have also raided flower gardens that still might have a few flowers blossoming, or visited with friends who might have had a hothouse.

They would have gathered the flowers in small baskets or bushels, and then returned home to decorate.

"Traditional decorations included holly and evergreens. The decoration of homes was not just for the gentry; poor families also brought greenery indoors to decorate their homes, but not until Christmas Eve. It was considered unlucky to bring greenery into the house before then. By the late 18th century, kissing boughs and balls were popular, usually made from holly, ivy, mistletoe and rosemary. These were often also decorated with spices, apples, oranges, candles or ribbons. In very religious households, the mistletoe was omitted," wrote historian Ben Johnson on HistoricUK.com.

The church did approve of holly, which it identified with the crown of thorns of Christ. Therefore, the hanging of holly in the house was thought to represent a more religious aspect to the practice. Being the daughters of a reverend, it is highly likely that Jane and Cassandra would have searched high and low for some holly in their region. Perhaps their grounds held some, or they knew of friends who might have holly growing on their estate, a perfect excuse for an early season visit.

"The aromatic leaves of bay, rosemary, ivy and yew . . . grace the stately fireplaces, while garlands, swags and wreaths made from holly . . . dress the sweeping staircase, as a reminder of the Crown of Thorns," reported the *Bristol Post*. Jane and Cassandra might have picked up fresh bay and rosemary from a still growing herb garden, perhaps even their own, or found them at the garden of a neighbor or a local market. Downstairs in the bustling kitchens, kissing bows and bunches of mistletoe might hang to add a touch of festivity to the scullery maid's day. To be sure, while the Austens were not wealthy, they were not poor either, and had a small staff of servants and a cook in their own household.

Wakefield points out, "It was not just grand houses that were decorated; as Cesar de Saussure commented, 'On this festival day churches, the entrances of houses, rooms, kitchens and halls are decked with laurels, rosemary and other greenery.'"

Fresh fruits were used as decoration as well, adding sweet smells to the different rooms. Apples, oranges and lemons were especially prized, as they were a show of wealth, indicating that the family either had a hot house or had acquired out-of-season fruit at a great expense.

In the time of the Austens, "the holiday was spent by the gentry in their country houses and estates, as they did not return to London until February. It was a time of high celebration with visiting, gift and charity giving, balls, parties, masquerades, play acting, games and lots of food. Since

Letters of Jane Austen

families and friends were already gathered together, it was also a time for courtships and weddings," wrote Boyle. Jane and Cassandra loved visiting friends, no matter how near or far, in the same manner, during this time of year. Their letters exist because they often visited friends and relatives separately during the season, and kept each other abreast of the news by way of their missives.

"In a tradition brought from Europe, St. Nicholas day was celebrated with the exchanging of small gifts among friends. Though it lacked the elaborate rituals found in the Netherlands (shoes and a multitude of presents for the children) it marked the official beginning of the Christmas Season," Boyle wrote. Jane and Cassandra might have exchanged presents, or they might have exchanged small gifts with friends from neighboring houses.

"After that, guests would arrive and the round of visiting, parties and balls would begin," continued Boyle. This is where Jane and Cassandra shared much fun, playing either the role of guest, or hostess. "So many guests required that a tremendous amount of food be kept on hand. Recipes which could be made ahead and served cold were popular with cooks and became the basis for many traditional recipes. Black Butter and Souse were a must as were a variety of meats, jellies and puddings. For Christmas dinner there was always a turkey, goose, or mutton, though venison held pride of place. Afterwards, of course, there was Christmas (or Plum) pudding ablaze in brandy sauce."

"From 1785 to 1787, Jane and her sister, Cassandra, attended a boarding school for girls, the Abbey School in Reading. When she came home, formal education had ended but learning had not," wrote scholar John Lauber.

Indeed, Jane was instructed in and excelled at both embroidery and sewing. As they grew older, it was clear that Cassy's talents lay in drawing and painting. Jane also played the piano.

The Austen family was a substantial one. Not only did she have her constant companion Cassy (born 1773) but she also had six brothers, James (born 1765), George (born 1766), Edward (born 1767), Henry Thomas (born 1771), Francis (Frank) William (born 1774), and Charles John (born 1779).

With everyone at home for the holidays, the Steventon Rectory must have been a bustling household. By all accounts, the home, with several ad hoc additions and wings, was a beehive of activity and chatter.

One can almost see it, as Jane later described in Mansfield Park, "Here everybody was noisy, every voice was loud (excepting, perhaps, her mother's, which resembled the soft monotony of Lady Bertram's, only worn into fretfulness). Whatever was wanted was hallooed for, and the servants hallooed out their excuses from the kitchen. The doors were in constant banging, the stairs were never at rest, nothing was done without a clatter, nobody sat still, and nobody could command attention when they spoke."

"Reading aloud in the family circle—fiction and non-fiction—was a favorite amusement of the time and practiced regularly by the Austens," wrote Lauber. Reverend Austen had a rich library filled with books of all kinds. From the time that Jane and Cassy could read well enough, their father's library was open to them with little editing. "Although a clergyman, George Austen has no puritanical prejudice against the theater, and plays might be read aloud or even performed, with productions improvised by the family and friends in the drawing room . . . " added Lauber.

During the Christmastide break, with everyone at home,

and visiting guests, it was a sure thing that these episodes were common in the Austen house. As young girls, Jane and Cassy were probably not the featured thespians, but these home theatricals were sure to make their mark on the budding young writer.

"The Austens were not only a lively and affectionate family, but an unusually literate one as well," continued Lauber.

Now to the mix would be added their famous aunt, her infamous daughter, and her daughter's newborn child.

"The Rectory was certainly too small a 'mansion' to contain the Comtesse and her mother, in addition to its own large family party and various pupils," recalled Jane's nephew, William Austen-Leigh.

"They eventually continued on to London, and just before Christmas, Eliza and her mother arrived at Steventon with the fat, fair baby and a gift for Jane, whose eleventh birthday was on December 16th. The present was a set of books in French called *L'ami des enfants* and is dated December 18th 1786 in each volume," wrote Spence. She arrived with numerous trunks, her mother, her pug dog, and an infant. She was a whirlwind all by herself.

The books had been inscribed to Jane, mostly from her aunt, reading in volume one, "Pour dear Jane Austen." "The affectation of mixing French and English catches something of both the women's style—the fashionable French 'pour' and the affectionate and familiar English 'dear,'" continued Spence. "Jane was entranced . . . [S]he was surprised that her glamorous cousin seemed entranced with her."

"I could not look forward without fear and trembling to the arrival of my great cousin, whom, with the levity of youth, I declared I was sure I would never like," recalled Janes brother, James Austen, who later wrote a fictitious account of the visit, from a young girl's point of view. "For the elegance of her dress, the complacency of her smile, and the easy politeness of her manner . . . operated so effectively in her favor, that before she had been in the house three days, I gave it as my opinion that she was the sweetest woman in the world."

There is no doubt that James was right on target. The reuniting of these women would have a major influence on Jane's writing. She is generally considered to be the inspiration for Lady Susan and the model for Mary Crawford, of Mansfield Park.

"[Upon] the arrival [of] Christmas, 1786," wrote novelist Carol Shields, "the household at Steventon was transformed during the visit of these exotic relations by a dose of French worldliness that affected all the Austens . . . French manners, French books, [and] French attitudes widened the intellectual and social reach of the family, en-livening daily life."

Eliza was a lightning rod at Steventon. Not only were her flirtatious ways constantly on display, but her suppos-edly scandalous background proceeded her always. "That Christmas, the Countess was especially conscious of her own status as the unacknowledged daughter of a great man. While they acted out their comedic dramas in the barn, or played charades around the fireside, the man whom she believed to be her father waited trial," wrote Austen biog-rapher David Nokes.

Philadelphia Austen had gone to India to marry Tysoe Saul Hancock in 1753. Due to slanderous rumors circulated at the time by a woman named Jenny Strachey, it had been rumored that Eliza was actually the natural child of Warren Hastings, who later became the first Governor-General of Bengal and the first Governor-General of India. At the time Hastings was embroiled in political turmoil and his name was much in the news. The Austens followed Hastings's struggles with intense curiosity.

Indeed, Eliza loved to perform in the Austen family the-atricals, as she often played leading lady. It is generally con-sidered that the Austens' cousin Philadelphia Walter, the daughter of William Hampson Walter, refused to come to

Steventon with Eliza to take part in some of these plays. The supposition is that she disapproved of Eliza's behavior.

Phylly Walter was a timid young woman who was modest and conservative, the polar opposite of the well-traveled and outgoing Eliza. "It afforded Eliza the greatest pleasure imaginable to tease and shock their timid cousin," wrote Nokes. For her part, Phylly had come to the conclusion that Eliza's mother was a model of sobriety and a model of perfection, while Eliza was something else altogether. "Between them there existed a kind of rivalry which provoked some lively disputes."

"Eliza fitted into the Steventon family circle, entering their spirited conversations and playing for them everyday—the Austens had borrowed a piano for her," wrote Spence.

"Eliza obtained Phylly's reluctant consent that together they should petition their Austen cousins to perform at the Rectory that Christmas," wrote Nokes, of that Christmas in 1876. "Thanks to James, the barn at Steventon was fitted up quite like a theater . . . [A]ll the young folks would have parts, James, Henry, and Francis, Cassandra and Jane, and of course, Phylly."

Though Jane's mother was somewhat vexed about the arrangements for such a gathering, she approved of the Christmastide theatrics. Phylly, however, was less inclined to participate. "I should like to be a spectator, but I am sure I should not have courage to act a part," she wrote. Jane's mother had written to timid Phylly that, fortunately, there was only room enough for "a place to hide your head in."

But Eliza was a force to be reckoned with, assuring Phylly that, "We shall have a most brilliant party and a great deal of amusement . . . the house full of company and frequent balls. You cannot possibly resist so many temptations especially when I tell you that your old friend James is returned from France and is to be of the acting party."

Eventually, Phylly reneged, and she could not be persuaded to attend. But the rest of the Austen clan was fully engaged and present. One can only imagine the rambling series of rooms in the old parsonage fully stocked with a trio of adults, and a school room's worth of young adults and children. Filled to bursting with a compliment of maids, cooks, and farm hands, as well as guests, Steventon must have been bustling as Christmas neared. Breakfasts and dinners with tables full of squabbling and cackling children. An abundance of food. Beds packed like sardines. Jokes, laughter, arguments. Piano playing. Nights spent by the fireplace with readings, games, and recitations. All in close quarters.

"The first and strongest impression the real Eliza made was that she was playful and unaffected. She made it her business to be agreeable to everyone, and Jane was not the only member of the family who was captivated by her," wrote Spence. "Henry had a special place at Steventon that Christmas. He was the only young man for Eliza to flirt with . . . Henry was not yet sixteen but was tall and good looking, and his height gave him the appearance of being a young man, so he was an acceptable target for Eliza. Flirtation was one of Eliza's greatest pleasures—she called it a 'trade.'"

Eliza's presence added an electric spark to the household. And Eliza's charms were not wasted on Jane's brother James either, who was also smitten with her. While Eliza may have had fun flirting with the young Henry, she did not consciously flirt with the older James. James was already twenty-three and had just recently been ordained. There was some tension between the two young men, both of whom wanted to play opposite of her in the theatricals. James, a self-styled poet, wrote many set pieces, and gave Eliza some fairly scintillating lines to deliver on the stage.

"In the end Henry got the part, and he and Eliza began rehearsals of their love scenes. Acting the parts meant they embraced and touched; Henry even got to kiss Eliza's hand," wrote Spence. "James had to endure the jealousy aroused by watching it all and knowing a covert romance was going on under the guise of acting."

As Spence pointed out, "There were two ways of looking at what went on during the theatricals: the French way—a married woman was seducing her sixteen year old cousin; and the English way—two young men were making fools of themselves over their married cousin."

Regardless, many of the young people in the house admired her. And as time wore on, her influence on Jane and her work would only grow.

Eliza de Feuillide was in fact the greatest and most lasting Christmas present of 1786. But this was not the last Christmas in which Eliza would play an important part.

1794

PART TWO: 1794

s the weather turned cold that December, Christmastide 1794 was to be a special year, though from outward appearances it could not have possibly looked very good.

England was now at war with France, and it had come home to the Austen family. Henry, Jane's favorite brother, had left his studies in February 1793, giving up his plan to become a clergyman like his father, and instead signed up as a "Gentleman to be Lieutenant" with the Oxford Militia. He then began a seven-year stint as an officer in the British army. He had been stationed at various places: Brighton, Ipswich, and Dublin. Henry found being an officer much more interesting than being a parson, and Jane loved to see Henry in his uniform; she thought he looked splendid. But things were not good in France, and the revolution there had already left bloody footprints on the Austens' front door.

That Christmastide, Eliza reappeared at Steventon. She was always welcomed and much loved. But her return during the early months of the year was altogether different. Where she had once been a divine, devilish, effervescent youth and new mother, with exciting fashion and a newborn babe, she now showed up a war refugee and widow.

Eliza had been living on the Rue de Grenelle-Saint Honoré in Paris with her husband, French Army Captain, Jean-François Capot de Feuillide, and their maidservant Rose Clarisse. In February of 1794, the captain was arrested.

"When [de Feuillide's] friend la Marquise de Marbeouf was arrested for planting grains instead of potatoes on her estate near Meux, Comte de Feuillide tried to bribe a man named Morel to release her. Morel worked for the Public Safety Committee; he led the Comte on, and had him arrested on 16th Pluviose and thrown into a Conciergerie cell," wrote Austen biographer Park Honnan.

"Eliza had been forced to watch in horror as the agents of the Committee pawed through all their household belongings. In the pocket of de Feuillide's trousers they found a receipt for 14,000 livres payable to the bearer and signed by Morel," wrote David Nokes. "Documents were impounded, money was confiscated . . . "

On February 22nd, 1794, Morel testified against de Feuillide at his trial. In an attempt to possibly save himself, the captain testified "to have sworn that he was only a poor, scheming, patriotic valet who had murdered the real Comte de Feuillide . . . "

According to Nokes, after Rose Clarisse and the housemaid both testified against him, "Eliza had even to endure the mortification of hearing de Feuillide's former mistress, la citoyenne Grandville, testifying against him."

Despite impassioned testimony by the Captain himself, he was declared guilty. "Jean Capot de Feuillide was condemned to death and guillotined within hours of his trial. Eliza's marriage had lasted for twelve years," wrote Claire Tomalin.

According to Honnan, Eliza was "Shocked, bemused and ill," which was understandable. To further complicate matters, the captain's admission that he was not the rightful Comte (whether true or not) had pre-empted Eliza from claiming any of the estates connected with the title. However, Warren Hastings, who was still wealthy despite his own trials, remained more than generous to his godchild, bestowing on her an ample lifestyle and allowance.

"To Jane, this whole ghastly pantomime of aristocrats pretending to be menials sounded like a grotesque parody," wrote Nokes of the Comte's charade.

"The Austens showed every kindness to Eliza, and Henry seemed particularly at pains to comfort her with the recent death of her husband, a newborn child to rear, and importuning Hastings for some allowance to live on until her own monies and properties could be sorted out," wrote Nokes. Eliza's emotions showed an inner turmoil when she first arrived. But whilst his attentions were flattering, Eliza was in no mood for flirtations and found greater solace in the sensible conversation of Jane and Cassandra, and the ever benevolent care of Mr. Austen," Nokes pointed out of Eliza soon after the episode in mid-1794.

Eliza was grateful to the Austens and was particularly fond of Reverend Austen, whom she "found congenial and comforting, sympathetic and devoted," remarked Honnan. Eliza had grown close to the Reverend after losing her mother, Philadelphia Hancock, to breast cancer a few years earlier. "Eliza always tenderly loved him; after poor Mrs. Hancock died of breast cancer Eliza simply sat for minutes looking into her uncle's gentle eyes until tears came to hers."

So here was Eliza, at Steventon for the holiday season, with snow falling, with her "brat" as she jokingly referred to him in letters, in tow. Henry and James were both enamored all over again. As the season wore on, Eliza was buoyed by the Austen family's care and affections. She seemingly regained her boisterous mood and jubilant spirit.

"But Eliza seemed too happy to run after young Henry Austen. They had quarreled before, and Henry had made up to her under the Austens' eyes at Steventon. Feeling free as an unfaded widow of thirty-four, she was flirting with a new passion for turning men into sheep and wives into harridans, though she usually admired the wives and understood a woman's obligation to another woman. Seldom in her letters is she unkind to any female," wrote Honnan. Still, she continued to be an inspiration to Jane.

Though Eliza would later become a huge influence on Jane's writings, Jane was already well on her way to writing before Eliza had come to stay with them. By this time Jane had already written the collection of works that would later be published as *Juvenilia*. "The earliest pieces probably date from 1786 or 1787, around the time, aged 11 or 12, that Jane Austen left the Abbey House School in Reading," wrote Kathryn Sutherland, Professor at St. Anne's College, University of Oxford. The later works in this collection were written in 1793, when she was seventeen and eighteen.

"Jane Austen's earliest writings appear to have little in common with the restrained and realistic society portrayed in her adult novels. By contrast, they are exuberantly expressionistic tales of sexual misdemeanor, of female drunkenness and violence. They are characterized by exaggerated sentiment and absurd adventures. Running through them is a pronounced thread of comment on and willful misreading of the literature of her day, showing how thoroughly and how early the activity of critical reading informed her character as a writer," continued Sutherland. "Common to all three notebooks is their portrayal of confident, willful, even rebellious young women: heroines like Charlotte Lutterell of 'Lesley Castle' (Volume the Second) and Catherine or Kitty, as she is usually styled, in the longer 'Kitty, or the Bower' in Volume the Third. Kitty is a more naturalistic figure than the farcical adventurers of the earlier tales but, like them, she is independent and outspoken."

The best-known works in *Juvenalia* are "The History of England," "Love and Friendship," "The Beautifull Cassandra," and "Memoirs of Mr. Clifford." Perhaps "History of England" is among the most famous for its prejudiced and sarcastic look at English history and for the wonderful and brilliantly colorful watercolors provided by Cassandra to augment the work.

"The Austens at any rate were surely touched by her 'History,' because its feelings mixed oddly with its jokes," wrote Honnan. "Jane Austen's romantic Toryism and half-mocking sympathy for Catholic royalty could not be taken as objectionable."

Portrait of Henry IV by Cassandra Austen, from "The History of England"

Jane preserved these early scribblings in three manuscript notebooks. They were entitled, with faux solemnity, "Volume the First," "Volume the Second," and "Volume the Third."

"Everything is from the hand of a confident and controlled stylist. The work shows sophisticated literary technique, so sophisticated that it is a temptation to say it wasn't mastered but came to her naturally. There is little awkward groping about as she tried to find her way," wrote Jon Spence. "What distinguishes the girl Jane Austen as much as her polished and controlled style is the refinement of her intellect. By the time she was eleven, she was a formidable rationalist."

"Jane Austen always distinguishes between true and spurious gentility, between internal worth and external rank or possession. Conventional gentility is founded on land and money . . . and the rich . . . are seldom examples of real worth and good breeding," wrote Douglas Bush, author of *Jane Austen (Masters of World Literature Series)*.

Scholars have often been amazed to examine Austen's earliest writings, as they show a young girl with a formidable wit, who was, if not wiser than her years, certainly more observant and insightful than many children her own age. Still, her writings, which were copious, showed a certain fancy for the fantastic.

"The girl was forever scribbling cruel and witty stories about people who shot each other, committed suicide or lost several of their limbs. And of course, the girl was in love (what girl of twelve is not?), or at least, as was usually the case, in love with the idea of being in love," wrote Nokes.

Jane's constant scribbling was not lost on Reverend Austen, a well-read man himself, who did as much as anyone to further Jane's interests in literature.

"Mr. Austen had long observed with approval his younger daughter's facility for literary composition," wrote Nokes, "and 12 [shillings] seemed to him a modest enough sum to invest in a talent which might prove, after all, to be nothing more than a source of ephemeral diversions." Nokes added that Reverend Austen had taken note of Jane's tendency toward flirtation by this point. "He considered it highly desirable that what he called her 'effusions of fancy' (which tended invariably to elopements and similar reckless adventures) should be confined to the pages of her manuscript book, and not acted out in real life."

"Mr. Austen, according to Eliza's letters, thought about very few topics unconnected with his family. He had broad interests, but children were the focal point, and Eliza might not have been astonished if anyone called him a successful father," opined Honnan. "His attitude was oddly easy and charitable."

It was with this generosity of spirit and a love for his youngest daughter that George Austen indulged Jane in her passion. He and she shared a love of books, but Reverend Austen was much taken with his daughter's desire to write. He intended to encourage it.

"For her nineteenth birthday, Mr. Austen bought Jane 'a small mahogany writing desk with 1 long drawer and glass ink stand compleat' which he purchased from Ring's of Bastingstoke for 12 [shillings]," wrote Nokes.

"This was a small but precious gift. While portable writing desks similar to Jane's were popular all through the 19th century, they did not become widespread until travel

18th-century portable writing desk

became more convenient for the middle and upper classes in the late 18th century. Writing boxes were versatile and portable and could easily be carried. They were placed on a table or one's lap, and were as personal as a diary, containing paper, pens, ink, and hidden compartments," explained Jane Austen expert Victoria Sanborn. "The wood rectangular box opened to reveal a sloped writing surface embossed in leather. Compartments stored writing implements like paper, pens, ink, stamps, sealing wax, etc."

Jane loved the desk, and it remained a very important part of her life until her death. There was one time when she was accidentally separated from it, which caused quite a stir.

Jane Austen wrote to her sister, Cassandra, years later, on Wednesday, October 24th, 1798, from the Bull and George at Dartford:

I should have begun my letter soon after our arrival but for a little adventure which prevented me. After we had been here a quarter of an hour it was discovered that my writing and dressing boxes had been by accident put into a chaise which was just packing off as we came in, and were driven away towards Gravesend in their way to the West Indies. No part of my property could have been such a prize before, for in my writing-box was all my worldly wealth, 7 lbs . . . Mr Nottley immediately dispatched a man and horse after the chaise and in half an hour's time I had the pleasure of being as rich as ever; they were got about two or three miles off.

This desk was to have immense importance in her life, and it marked a significant shift in her writing and attitude. Jane would begin many of her great works writing on this very desk.

"The first part of her writing career was over. She was no longer the precocious girl who wrote for the entertainment of her family and friends. She was a young woman of immense talent, brilliant gifts, potential genius," wrote Spence.

"Jane's reaction to this gift was a spirited piece of literary defiance. The first thing she wrote at her new desk only confirmed her fascination with the disruptive powers of flirtation," wrote Honnan.

The result of this gift paid immediate dividends, as Jane promptly sat down and began *Lady Susan* around 1794. An epistolary novel and complete work, *Lady Susan* was her most ambitious work to date.

"Jane drew on Eliza's exploits to write the novelette-in-letters," wrote Honnan. "Lady Susan had Eliza's gaiety and Jane's love of assertion and fondness for making things happen at nineteen and twenty . . . Certainly she admired Eliza's energy as a key to happiness . . . "

"Her earliest writings were filled with anarchic imaginings and cheerful violence, and her early novel *Lady Susan*, probably written when she was a teen-ager, uncannily echoes Laclos's scandalous novel *Les Liaisons Dangereuses*, featuring a dazzling female Don Juan as its protagonist. Austen's reading was apparently not censored by her parents: Richardson's *Sir Charles Grandison* was a favorite; so was Fielding's racy *Tom Jones*," wrote famed *New York Times* book critic Michiko Kakutani.

"Like most of her juvenile stories, it is about bad behavior; but it is finished and polished, sophisticated in its analysis of behavior, and quite unlike anything she had yet written or was ever to write again; an altogether extraordinary piece of work to come from the pen of a country clergyman's daughter," wrote Tomalin. "She creates a female predator who holds centre-stage throughout; and wittly tells her own story; her wickedness is real, but she is also attractive and so entertaining that we find ourselves sympathizing with her in her battle with the dullards who are her victims."

"The seductive language suggests the influence of the Comtesse de Feuillide. It was from Eliza that Jane had learnt the racy idioms of society flirtation. It was from Eliza that she heard of the dangerous excitement of sexual deceit. The language of Lady Susan is the language of Eliza," wrote Nokes.

"Lady Susan is sometimes associated with Eliza de Feuilide, and not only because she was a clever and beautiful young widow," wrote Tomalin. "The exercise is brilliant. So brilliant, that Austen may have frightened herself, and felt she had written herself into a dangerous corner, and been too clever, too bold, too black."

"*Lady Susan* is obliquely, even covertly, as much about Jane's relationship with Eliza as it is overtly about

Henry's," opined Spence. "Jane's immediate concern was for her brother, but she herself was troubled by Eliza. It appeared once Jane perceived the faults in Eliza's character, she withdrew from the intimate friendship that they had established—not so difficult because Eliza was an irregular correspondent and was taken up with Henry, not Jane."

In a similar vein, Jane had written another small piece entitled "Eliza and Henry." It was very much about their early flirtations. But it was soon becoming clear that Eliza and Henry would make a match. It must have vexed Jane to lose her favorite brother to such an independent and vivacious woman who she now thought of as a predator.

Over the next few years, Eliza, James, and Henry would perform a series of over-arching turns in their respective relationships. Eliza was clearly interested in Henry. But James had not lost his ardor for Eliza either. Henry pursued Eliza, but she was not yet ready to give up her freedom. When James proposed, she let him dangle for sometime, though it was clear she never intended to seriously consider him. After refusing him, he immediately proposed to someone else, and was soon thereafter married. However, it was clear that Henry was still very much on Eliza's mind.

No doubt, the series of parlor scenes involving Eliza, Henry, and James were not wasted on Jane, who most likely

Bringing in the Yule Log at Christmas, 1832, Chambers' Book of Days

thought the triangles that were forming might have seemed right out of a classic drawing-room comedy still popular in those days. This particular series of vignettes began to play out as the Christmas holiday encroached.

Being a family contented to stay within their own unit, one can only imagine the Austens honoring the traditions of the season. Jane and Cassandra had by now brought in the usual greenery. A seemingly conservative family, the Austens might have followed the tradition of the Yule log, which was still very much in the fashion those days.

"A great blazing fire was the centerpiece of a family Christmas. The Yule log was chosen on Christmas Eve. It was wrapped in hazel twigs and dragged home, to burn in the fireplace as long as possible through the Christmas season. The tradition was to keep back a piece of the Yule log to light the following year's Yule log," wrote historian Ben Johnson.

This was very much on old English country tradition, which might have been in keeping at Steventon and the surrounding estates.

"The grate had been removed from the wide overwhelming fireplace, to make way for a fire of wood, in the midst of which was an enormous log glowing and blazing, and sending forth a vast volume of light and heat; this I understood was the Yule-log, which the Squire was particular in having brought in and illumined on a Christmas eve, according to ancient custom," wrote Washington Irving in *Old Christmas* about his visit to a great English estate of the period.

"It was really delightful to see the old Squire seated in his hereditary elbow-chair by the hospitable fireside of his ancestors, and looking around him like the sun of a system, beaming warmth and gladness to every heart," Washington wrote of the experience. "Even the very dog that lay stretched at his feet, as he lazily shifted his position and yawned, would look fondly up in his master's face, wag his tail against the floor, and stretch himself again to sleep, confident of kindness and protection. There is an emanation from the heart in genuine hospitality which cannot be described, but is immediately felt, and puts the stranger at once at his ease. I had not been seated many minutes by the comfortable hearth of the worthy cavalier before I found myself as much at home as if I had been one of the family."

According to *Chambers Book of Days:*

The burning of the Yule log is an ancient Christmas ceremony, transmitted to us from our Scandinavian ancestors, who, at their feast of Juul, at the winter-solstice, used to kindle huge bonfires in honor of their god Thor. The custom, though sadly shorn of the 'pomp and circumstance' which formerly attended it, is still maintained in various parts of the country. The bringing in and placing of the ponderous block on the hearth of the wide chimney in the baronial hall was the most joyous of the ceremonies observed on Christmas Eve in feudal times. The venerable log, destined to crackle a welcome to all-comers, was drawn in triumph from its resting-place at the feet of its living brethren of the woods. Each wayfarer raised his hat as it passed, for he well knew that it was full of good promises, and that its flame would burn out old wrongs and hearthurnings, and cause the liquor to bubble in the wassail-bowl, that was quaffed to the drowning of ancient feuds and animosities. So the Yule-log was worthily honored, and the ancient bards welcomed its entrance with their minstrelsy.

"Welcome Yule," a ditty appropriate to such an occasion, appears in the Sloane Manuscripts. It is supposed to be of the time of Henry VI:

Welcome be thou, heavenly King,
Welcome born on this morning,
Welcome for whom we shall sing,
    Welcome Yule.

Welcome be ye Stephen and John,
Welcome Innocents every one,
Welcome Thomas Martyr one,
                    Welcome Yule.

Welcome be ye, good New Year,
Welcome Twelfth Day, both in fere,
Welcome saints, loved and dear,
                    Welcome Yule.

Welcome be ye, Candlemas,
Welcome be ye, Queen of Bliss,
Welcome both to more and less,
                    Welcome Yule.

Welcome be ye that are here,
Welcome all, and make good cheer,
Welcome all, another year,
                    Welcome Yule.

This would have been a Christmas carol with which the Austens were familiar.

And here, in connection with the festivities on Christmas Eve, we may quote Herrick's inspiring stanzas:

Come bring with a noise,
My merry, merry boys,
*   The Christmas log to the firing,*
While my good dame she
Bids ye all be free,
*   And drink to your heart's desiring.*

With the last year's brand
Light the new block, and,
*   For good success in his spending,*
On your psalteries play
That sweet luck may
*   Come while the log is a-teending.*

Drink now the strong beer,
Cut the white loaf here,
*   The while the meat is a shredding;*
For the rare mince-pie,
And the plums stand by,
*   To fill the paste that's a kneading.*

One can almost see the Austens settled in against the cold nights, with the fire blazing, playing their games of charades or reading aloud to one another. If not hard spirits, the Austens might have sipped mulled wine, cider, or even beer during these moments. Other traditions abounded. Celebrating the season with light was a popular custom.

"As an accompaniment to the Yule log, a candle of monstrous size, called the Yule Candle, or Christmas Candle, shed its light on the festive-board during the evening evening," wrote author Nathan Boughton Warren. "[John] Brand, in his in his *Popular Antiquities*, states that, in the buttery of St. John's College, Oxford, an ancient candle socket of stone still remains, ornamented with the figure of the Holy Lamb. It was formerly used for holding the Christmas Candle, which, during the Twelve Nights of the Christmas festival, was burned on the high-table at supper."

Contrary to the day of Jane's birth, snow was not normally a problem at this time of year for the Reverend and his family.

"You did not necessarily have to worry about snow near Christmas, despite the story of Good King Wenceslas. According to several sources, weather in most parts of England is often warm and damp over Christmas. A notable exception is the Christmas of 1813, which was unusually cold. The famous Frost Fair that froze the Thames was the following January. However, near New Years, the weather generally turns colder, so that skating and sledding become possible," wrote historical novelist Regina Scott.

The Austens were a church-going family. Christmas day would have begun with Reverend Austen going to the Steventon church, accompanied by his wife, and dutiful sons and daughters. The family might have helped arrange the church or decorate it modestly for the season. Indeed, Jane and Cassandra might have brought greens or small bouquets with them on their walk for just such purposes. After services, the family might linger and chat with parishioners, possibly stopping along the way back to visit friends in the village, before completing the trek back to their parsonage.

For the lay person, "Christmas Day might start with a trip to church, followed by a lavish dinner of boar's head, which was really the head of a pig, as wild boars became extinct in England approximately 1185. You might also have turkey (which had been brought to England from the New World in 1550), along with plum pudding, march pane (what we often call marzipan), and gingerbread. Christmas Day was also the day on which a gift or tithe was given to the landowner. Note, however, it was not a widespread tradition to give each other gifts. Again, period diaries indicate it was more common to give a new toy to the children in the family than for the adults to exchange gifts," wrote Scott.

One can only imagine that Christmas, with Henry and James renewing their younger rivalry over an older woman. The duel pitted the stalwart clergyman and the young, tall, rakish army officer easily remind one of Austen's later characters from *Pride and Prejudice*. It must have seemed like parson William Collins vying for the attentions of Elizabeth Bennet versus Mr. George Wickham.

The old house must still have had some bustle to it. Older siblings had married and borne children. While the house may no longer have had the horde of people and children as it did in the old days, still, there was enough drama and tension to fill a small soap opera. James and Henry were no longer little tykes. Both were men now, as the Christmas season came and went. With all the greenery and mistletoe, it must have been like a Sheridan play set on a Christmas set, with the two of them mooning over the wicked Eliza.

In the end, Henry and Eliza did marry, in December of 1797. But that was another Christmas.

For now Jane was a young woman, who was beginning to understanding her powers as a writer...and as a woman. In future yuletide seasons, Jane would be much more the star of her own life and experience her own intrigues. But Eliza's influence would extend for many years to come.

1795

PART THREE: 1795

Christmastide of 1795 was a highlight for the twenty-year-old Jane Austen not only because it heralded the start of the ball season, but because it was the meeting of the first great love of her life.

But first we must start at the beginning. An important person in Jane's life was "Mrs. Lefroy, wife of the Reverend Isaac Lefroy, Rector of Ashe, living in a spacious elegant house a few miles from Steventon. She was known in the district as Madam Lefroy; the designation suggests that she was recognized as deserving to be distinguished from the ordinary run of commonplace people," wrote literary historian David Cecil. "Madam Lefroy was a personality, gifted and considerable . . . Animated, enthusiastic and with a winning manner, she was an admirable hostess and must have had an unusually perceptive eye for quality in others; for she was the first person of whom we have record to notice that there was something special about Jane Austen. She had her often to her house, sympathized with her, encouraged her and drew her out. To be singled out for special notice by an attractive older man or woman is a great event in an intelligent young person's life."

As Claire Tomalin pointed out, "[Jane] was already greatly admired among the many gentlemen of the neighborhood, and it was to become a moot point with her whether flirtation or novel-writing afforded her greater delight. On the whole, she rather inclined to believe that it must be flirtation . . . " She had been the recipient of many flirtations, including a request for a kiss from a young man known as C. Powlett, and was the object of several other young men's affections.

According to the Historic Odessa Foundation, "The Christmas season in Georgian/Regency England was a festive time of the year which inevitably diverted one's attention away from the cold and dark months of winter. The early 1800's presented a time of entertainment with evening balls, parlor games, and family parties. The rooms in the house were interpreted to show visitors both the celebration side of the holidays and the preparation side of the home-owners and their servants."

Vignette of a traditional Georgian Christmas feast, Historic Odessa Foundation of Delaware

The highlight of the Christmastide season for adults, especially young adults, was the series of dances and balls given during the season.

"In reality, Austen loved balls, which were the most exciting events in provincial life," wrote literary historian John Mullan.

In those days, "there was no set way for a young lady to make her debut in society," wrote Austen expert Martha C. Sullivan. Her parents might throw a ball in her honor, "or she might start attending dinners and evening parties with her parents. In many families it was common for the eldest daughter to at least be engaged before the youngest daughters were allowed to come out, presumably so they would not compete with her for potential husbands or embarrass her by becoming engaged first."

"Modern readers are sometimes puzzled as to why dance scenes have so prominent a place in Jane Austen's novels; but in her lifetime the dance floor was the best, and indeed the only place, where marriage partners could be identified and courtship could flourish," wrote Jane Austen authority Deirdre Le Faye.

"In Austen's fiction, as in many novels of the 19th century, a ball is the ultimate occasion for a heady kind of courtship—a trying out of partners that is exciting, flirtatious and downright erotic. Couples perform together, feeling each other's physical proximity (though both men and women wore gloves throughout) while being watched by others," wrote Mullan.

These series of balls, especially of this season of 1795, became very important in Jane's fiction. "Nowhere is the combination of realism and metaphor more clearly shown than in her use of the dance. It is possible to reconstruct many of the social customs of the age simply by studying the descriptions of the balls and dances in *Emma*, in *Mansfield Park*, in *Pride and Prejudice*, and even in *Northanger Abbey*; but it is also possible to see the ritualized encounters of the ballrooms as indicators of social and sexual definition," wrote Austen scholar Alice Chandler.

There were distinct differences between the gatherings. Some were public dances or assemblies, where anyone could pay a fee for entrance.

"Public assemblies usually require[d] the payment of a fee, which your father [would] remit on your behalf. If you [attended] a series of balls at the same establishment, your father [could] obtain for you a subscription allowing you to attend for the season," wrote Sullivan.

On the other hand, private balls, by invitation only, were much more prestigious and showy affairs. While dances and balls might be given throughout the year, the Christmastide season saw a rush of them during the month-long celebrations in the country.

"Whether an elegant ball at a grand house, a village assembly, or in the drawing room after dinner, dancing play[ed] a vital role in the Regency social scene," wrote Sullivan.

"Dressing for a ball [was] part of the fun," Sullivan continued. "White muslin [was] always [an] appropriate and fashionable choice for a young lady, adorned with a simple cross pendant on a gold chain, or perhaps pearls from your mother. Pin back you hair with beads, flowers, or feathers woven through," continued Sullivan in *The Jane Austen*

Handbook, a detailed how-to guide for emulating ballroom fashion, "but allow a few curls to fall around your face."

Jane and Cassandra, not unlike other women of the day, were keen to be in step with the latest fashion trends and would either altar existing clothes or purchase new ones. "...next week shall begin my operations on my hat," Jane once wrote Cassandra, "on which you know my principal hopes of happiness rely."

Even as late as 1814, Jane told Cassandra in a letter, "I have been ruining myself in black sattin ribbon with a proper perl edge; & now I am trying to draw it up into kind of Roses, instead of putting it in plain double plaits."

As was the custom then, ladies usually slept in a little later on the morning before a ball, so that they might reserve their energy for the festivities. It was also generally thought by women not to eat too much before or at a ball, as one did not want to appear lethargic at the event, but rather to seem light, springy, and spritely.

"Codes of behavior were exacting," wrote Mullan. For example, women were not allowed to dance with strangers at a public assembly. Thus, if a man wanted to dance with a woman he did not know, he needed to be introduced to that woman. "Propriety demands that he seek an introduction from the master of ceremonies or a mutual acquaintance before he requests your company at a dance," wrote Sullivan. If a young lady was to dance with a stranger, her reputation might be ruined. However, at a private ball, by invitation only, it was acceptable for a young lady to dance with a gentleman she did not know.

Jane illustrates an example of this in *Pride and Prejudice*, when Elizabeth Bennet is approached by Mr. Collins.

"At the Netherfield ball Elizabeth must dance with Mr. Collins because if a woman turns down one request for a dance she must turn down all others. Say no to Mr. Collins and you must stand out for the whole evening. Elizabeth's first two dances (the maximum you were allowed with the same partner) are therefore 'dances of mortification.' Mr. Collins, 'often moving wrong without being aware of it', gives her 'all the shame and misery which a disagreeable partner for a couple of dances can give' (ch. 18). He, of course, thinks that he has done brilliantly, the dance being a preparation for his proposal of marriage the next day," wrote Mullan.

Jane was an enthusiastic participant. One December she wrote to Cassandra that she had danced twenty dances "without any fatigue—I was glad to find myself capable of being able to dance so much & with so much satisfaction as I did . . ."

Jane and Cassandra kept up on the latest dances, and were eager to spend their time on the floor. But it was also physically exhausting.

"Many of the dances were physically demanding: a ball might last for six hours or more, and end only as dawn approached (in *Sense and Sensibility*, Marianne is delighted to hear of Willoughby dancing 'from eight o'clock till four, without once sitting down.') In a crowded room lit by candles the heat could be overwhelming. When you are told in *Pride and Prejudice* that Mr. Bingley 'danced every dance' at the Meryton assembly ball you should realise that he is a thoroughly vigorous young man," wrote Mullan.

Jane turned her ballroom experiences, as well as Cassandra's, into prose. They both wanted not only to enjoy the dances, but of course, to prove themselves graceful and promising partners for the eligible young men of the area. These desires come across in much of Jane's work.

"The patterns of steps and movements were often compli-
cated and required a great deal of practice. Books were published to guide would-be dancers. Look at these patterns and
you might sympathise with Mr. Collins for his incompetence.
Even the Bennet girls, whose education was entirely neglect-
ed by their mother, would have had lessons. Dancing well was
a test, and when Austen's heroines take the floor with the
men they love it is in order to perform well together. Dancing
is one of the female 'accomplishments' that Miss Bingley lists
during Elizabeth's earlier stay at Netherfield. When her fellow
dancers at the Netherfield Ball see Elizabeth take the floor
with Mr. Darcy, they are suitably in awe. As she stands opposite him, she reads 'in her neighbours' looks' their 'amaze-
ment.' They are in awe because of his social status, and because he has chosen to dance with one of the local girls. Some
of the other young ladies will also have to come into contact
with him as they prance and rotate," concluded Mullan.

Christmastide provided a rather intense four to six week period wherein dances and balls were plentiful, and young people engaged heavily during that period. It was a heady experience for a young woman. And of course for Jane, this was also the time of her birthday, adding extra excitement to the festivities of the season.

"Balls were regarded as social experiences, and gentlemen were tasked to dance with as many ladies as they could. This is one reason why Mr. Darcy's behavior was considered rude at the Meryton Ball—there were several ladies, as Elizabeth pointed out to him and Colonel Fitzwilliam at Rosings, who had to sit out the dance," wrote Jane Austen authority Victoria Sanborn.

"He danced only four dances, though gentlemen were scarce; and, to my certain knowledge, more than one young lady was sitting down in want of a partner," said our heroine Ms. Bennet.

"Mr. Bingley, on the other hand, danced every dance and thus behaved as a gentleman should," concluded Sandborn. "Regency dances were extremely lively. The dancers were young, generally from 18-30 years of age, and they did NOT slide or glide sedately, as some recent film adaptations seem to suggest. They performed agile dance steps and exerted themselves in vigorous movements which included hopping, jumping, skipping, and clapping hands."

Contrary to what many movies have portrayed, the dances then were fast-paced and required lightness of foot. Many movies have used dances from previous generations, being slower, to make staging and filming easier.

"In the 18th and early 19th century, walking was not considered dancing. The music was lively (jigs and reels), and the dances were performed primarily by people in their late teens and early twenties (not known for their sedate habits). There were actual dance steps, and demonstrating the ability to perform them well was an important aspect of the dancing," wrote music and dance historian Susan de Guardiola.

In the early part of the Regency, including the early 1810s, the ballroom was dominated by three dances: the country dance, the cotillion, and the scotch reel.

Regency country dances were often begun by a brief march by the couples down the room. Then the lady at the top of the line would, with her partner, dance down to the bottom during the course of the set. In a country dance, couples in a line would perform a series of figures, dancing with and around one another, progressing up and down the line.

"One element mostly abandoned in modern country dancing is the top-down progression of the dance. Today there is a great emphasis on maximizing the time every person in the set spends dancing. This was not the case two hundred years ago. Dances were not started with everyone moving simultaneously," wrote Susan de Guardiola. "Instead, the first couple in a set would begin while all the rest watched to see what the dance would be." This was a position of honor and responsibility, an opportunity for that couple to show off the excellence of their steps and set the standard for the other dancers, as Fanny does in *Mansfield Park*:

> '...and she found herself the next moment conducted by Mr. Crawford to the top of the room, and standing there to be joined by the rest of the dancers, couple after couple, as they were formed.'

"As the couple worked their way down a long set of dancers (this could take ten minutes or more), additional dancers would join in, until the entire set was moving," continued Ms. de Guardiola. "When the lead couple reached the bottom, they would stand out briefly before rejoining the dance to assist the other couples progressing down the set. Time spent not dancing was not considered wasted time or 'just standing around'; it was a rare opportunity for intimate, unchaperoned conversation with one's partner. On a practical level, it also provided time to catch one's breath after the several minutes of vigorous non-stop dancing involved in moving down the set."

The cotillion was imported from France. Performed in a square or circle, it featured elaborate footwork. One danced a series of ten standard 'changes' and then the eleventh change or 'chorus' was unique. Many of the standard ten steps were rather simple and easy to emulate once observed.

In the Regency period, the scotch reel was a series of alternate interlacing figures complimented by fancy steps danced in place, all done in a line of three or four dancers.

"Boulangers, or circular dances, were performed at the end of the evening, when the couples were tired. Jane Austen danced the boulanger, which she mentioned in a letter to Cassandra in 1796: 'We dined at Goodnestone, and in the evening danced two country-dances and the Boulangeries,'" wrote Sanborn.

For her part, it is very likely Jane never danced the quadrille or the waltz, both of which came into fashion toward the end of her life, much later in the Regency period. In fact, the waltz was introduced in the Prince Regent's court by a foreign diplomat's wife of questionable reputation, and was thought lewd by public standards in Jane's lifetime.

"The earliest of Jane's letters to survive was addressed to Cassandra, wishing her a happy birthday. Jane wrote it sitting at home in her father's parsonage on Saturday, January 9th, 1796, and it is a remarkable document," wrote Tomalin. "Cassandra was away from home for the Christmas of 1795, staying with her future in-laws the Fowles in Berkshire. She was there to cheer them and be cheered in turn." Her intended, Tom Fowle, was in Falmouth awaiting to be shipped to the West Indies.

During the Christmastide season of 1795, over the course of four balls, Austen would meet the young, dashing, Thomas Langlois Lefroy. Lefroy was born in Limerick, Ireland. At Trinity College, Dublin, he had achieved a remarkable academic record in the years between 1790 and 1793. He next engaged in his legal studies, in Lincoln's Inn, London, under the guidance of his great-uncle, Benjamin Langlois, who sponsored Tom. After completing these studies, Lefroy became Auditor of the College Historical Society at Trinity.

In the Christmastide of 1795, Tom Lefroy went to the country to spend the holiday with his aunt, Madam Lefroy. During the course of that season, and during four balls given in that time, a romance took place that would mark Austen's writings for the rest of her life. And Lefroy himself would become a character who would be recycled and reinvented several times over.

"[Madam Lefroy] soon introduced him to Jane Austen, perhaps at Ashe or at the Harwood's Ball," wrote Park Honan. "Jane was then slender and agile and quick, a born dancer, with beautiful sparkling eyes and reddish healthy cheeks which made her less self-conscious . . . "

"He is very gentlemanlike, good looking, pleasant young man, I assure," Jane wrote to Cassandra.

"Tom and Jane met at four balls during his stay at Ashe," Madam Lefroy's home, wrote Jon Spence. "Their attraction seems to have been immediate."

"You could make of Tom what you wanted and that was his lovely charm. He seemed superficially to be a malleable dummy—except in formal debate," wrote Honan. "He would be twenty on January 8th; he [had] the foxy-colored hair of Lefroy males, with perhaps not enough glint to be called 'Yellow Cockatoo' as a descendant was; but his portrait taken in the new year suggests he wore powder, and shows his then clear blue, alert, and oddly innocent eyes . . . He was tidy and immaculate," wrote Honan.

Lefroy was conscious of his Irish accent, and was bashful of speaking too much. "Jane responded to his stupid silences; she admired his conservative air. She had much in common with him in outlook. A political novelist might have put them together. She had decided to fall in love, and saw little at any time to make her regret that decision," opined Honan.

"They both knew that Tom's time in Hampshire was limited. His family in Ireland had great ambitions for him as a lawyer, and his visit to Ashe was designed merely as a short holiday, for the good of his health, before he resumed his legal studies," wrote David Nokes. "Although she had known Tom Lefroy for barely a few weeks, their intimacy was already the talk of the neighborhood."

Jane and Tom were acutely aware of the gossip surrounding

Tom Lefroy

their romance. So much so, that when Jane went to visit Madam Lefroy during that season, Tom, embarrassed by the ribbing he'd taken regarding their intimacy, ran out of the house before she arrived.

"All suggests that her Irish lover accepted his assigned role. "If she'd done all the running, as a Lefroy descendent states, she did it only at first. We happen to know Tom came to Steventon once when she did not expect him," Honan wrote.

"Jane heard a knock at the Rectory door. There was Tom Lefroy, accompanied by his brother George. Her pleasure at seeing him was so great the she could only control it by recourse to her familiar defense of literary mockery. His coat was a great deal too light in color, she complained. But then, what could one expect of a man who was such a professed admirer of Tom Jones," wrote Nokes.

At the Harwood's Ball, the two were together constantly.

"Nobody forces a young man to dance and even a boulanger survives if he sits one out; and Tom chose her again and again, and, marked her name on his card and she did his on hers," wrote Honan of their meeting at the Harwood's Ball.

"Wine at the Harwood's flowed easily, and the rich, plentiful food with soups, fish, fowls, pies, chickens, jellies, cream, fruit, and custards kept everyone else occupied," wrote Honan.

In a lively letter to Cassandra on January 9th, 1796, Jane describes a ball at the Bigg-Wither's house, Manydown:

> Mr. Heathcote began with Elizabeth, and afterwards danced with her again; but they do not know how to be particular. I flatter myself, however, that they will profit by the three successive lessons which I have given them.
>
> You scold me so much in the nice long letter which I have this moment received from you, that I am almost

afraid to tell you how my Irish friend and I behaved. Imagine to yourself everything most profligate and shocking in the way of dancing and sitting down together. I can expose myself, however, only once more, because he leaves the country soon after next Friday, on which day we are to have a dance at Ashe after all. He is a very gentlemanlike, good-looking, pleasant young man, I assure you. But as to our having ever met, except at the three last balls, I cannot say much; for he is so excessively laughed at about me at Ashe, that he is ashamed of coming to Steventon, and ran away when we called on Mrs. Lefroy a few days ago…After I had written the above, we received a visit from Mr. Tom Lefroy and his cousin George. The latter is really very well-behaved now; and as to the other, he has but one fault, which time will I trust entirely remove; it is that his morning coat is a great deal too light. He is a very great admirer of Tom Jones, and therefore wears the same colored clothes, I imagine, which he did when he was wounded.

"Jane's teasing admission—really, a boast—was not the first Cassandra had heard about her sister's flirtation with Tom, and she had evidently written to Jane warning her to be more restrained in her behavior. Jane laughed it off," wrote Jon

Spence. "She was in high spirits and even a scolding from Cassandra (if in fact it was serious) could not dampen her mood."

As Claire Tomalin pointed out, "The reference to Fielding's Tom Jones is another provocative remark. Jane is making clear that she doesn't mind talking about a novel which candidly and comically deals with sexual attraction, fornication, bastard children and the oily hypocrisy of parsons . . . By telling Cassandra she and Tom Lefroy have talked about the book together, she lets her know just how free and even bold their conversation has been."

A few days later Jane wrote again to Cassandra, reporting:

Our party to Ashe to-morrow night will consist of Edward Cooper, James (for a ball is nothing without him), Buller, who is now staying with us, and I. I look forward with great impatience to it, as I rather expect to receive an offer from my friend in the course of the evening. I shall refuse him, however, unless he promises to give away his white coat.

"But by Friday morning all her hopes had been tuned to ashes. The ball, to which she had looked forward to with such eager anticipation, would be a penance, not a pleasure. There would be no proposal from Tom Lefroy, no delicious tete-a-tete or secret understanding," wrote Nokes. "His family, taking sudden fright at the prospect of an engagement between this young penniless couple, had stepped in to prohibit any further contact between them."

"The crux of the matter may well have been that Lefroy was still a 'boy' when it came to serious commitment. His own family was poor; he was dependent on a wealthy uncle for his education; and he would be called to the Irish Bar," reasoned Oliver MacDonagh, a literary historian.

Lefroy himself knew "he could not be allowed to risk his future by entangling himself in a love affair with a penniless girl," wrote Tomalin.

"Mrs. Lefroy induced Tom to return to London 'as soon as possible,'" wrote MacDonagh.

"Her sons—one of them the George who called on Jane with Tom—said later that their mother sent Tom packing so 'that no more mischief might be done,' and that she blamed him 'because he had behaved so ill to Jane.' The implication is clear that Jane took his attention very seriously," wrote Claire Tomalin.

That Friday Jane wrote to Cassandra, "At length the day is come on which I am to flirt my last with Tom Lefroy, and when you receive this it will be over. My tears flow as I write at the melancholy idea."

"Tom's departure of Ashe on or about January 20th 1796 ended the matter for him. Not so with Jane," wrote MacDonagh.

"Truly the 'prim' little girl of twelve had made considerable progress by the time she was twenty!" wrote nephew William Austen-Leigh. "Unfortunately, there is no further letter to tell us whether Tom made the expected proposal or not; but it is pretty certain that he did not, and indeed there is a good deal of doubt whether it was really expected. Possibly lack of means prevented its ever being a serious matter on his side. They can never have met again on the same intimate terms."

"So Jane never saw Tom Lefroy again after his Christmas visit of 1795," wrote Tomalin. "A small experience, perhaps, but a painful one for Jane Austen, this brush with young Tom Lefroy. From now on she carried in her own flesh and blood, and not just gleaned from books and plays, the knowledge of sexual vulnerability; of what it is to be entranced by the dangerous stranger; to hope, to feel the blood warm; to wince, to withdraw; to long for what you are not going to have and had better not mention. Her writing becomes informed by this knowledge, running like a dark under-current beneath a comedy."

"No doubt the disappointment of this love affair galvanized feelings of vulnerability and defensiveness that Austen felt as a child," wrote book critic Michiko Kakutani in the

New York Times. "It was in the months after Lefroy's departure from Hampshire that Austen turned increasingly to writing.

For his part, Tom Lefroy disappeared from Jane's life, though he never forgot her till his death at the age of ninety. He had accomplished a distinguished career. He had married a woman of wealth and had a considerable career on the bench and in politics. He served as a Member of Parliament for the constituency of Dublin University in 1830–1841, Privy Councilor of Ireland in 1835–1869, and Lord Chief Justice of Ireland in 1852–1866.

When he was an old man he told a young relation that "he had been in love with Jane Austen, but it was 'a boyish love.'"

"Whatever his qualification means, his admission confirms that Jane was not mistaken: Tom Lefroy had been in love with her. But of no less significance than Tom's answer is the fact that the question was asked at all. You might expect a nephew to have asked if his uncle had known the novelist Jane Austen; that would have been a natural question. But to ask if Tom had been in love with her shows that the question had lingered in family lore for more than seventy years. That in itself tells us a lot," wrote Jon Spence. Possibly by coincidence, and possibly not, literary scholars have pointed out that Tom Lefroy's first daughter was named Jane Christmas Lefroy. The derivation of this name has been hotly debated. It is possible that the name Jane was derived from Lady Jane Paul (Tom's mother-in-law). Others have thought the name just too much of coincidence.

"Jane never again mentioned Tom Lefroy in her letters, at least not in any Cassandra kept," commented Spence. "She had loved Tom Lefroy and had waited for him but he had not come. There was no more to be said. It was as absolute as the death of Cassandra's fiancé. Jane probably thought of it in something like those terms. Many years later she told her niece Fanny that 'it is no creed of mine, as you must well be aware, that such sort of Disappointments kill anybody.' She had earned the right to say that…"

For her part, there is no question that Lefroy's exit was a painful experience. It has been thought that Lefroy might have served as one or both Mr. Darcy and Mr. Bingley. Bingley is spirited away by his family when he falls too easily in love with Jane Bennet in *Pride and Prejudice*. Jon Spence suggested that the inverted was true: that Jane was actually the role model for Mr. Darcy and Tom the role model for Ms. Bennet. Also, a similar situation appears in *Sense and Sensibility* when the young Mr. Bingley is suddenly whisked away.

Regardless, the Christmastide season of balls in 1795 would stay with Jane Austen the rest of her life, and inform her writings and characters for many years to come.

1802

PART FOUR: 1802

I n the beginning of December 1802, Jane and Cassandra headed for Manydown, the home of their friends, the Bigg sisters. Throughout that November, Jane and Cassandra had gone from house to house, visiting friends and relations in the country.

The sisters were both living in Bath at the time. The Reverend George Austen had formally retired in 1800, leaving the Steventon Rectory to James and his wife Mary, and moved there with his wife and daughters.

Jane hated Bath. She had found it interesting on her first visit, but she was not happy living there. "There was a monstrous deal of stupid quizzing and commonplace nonsense talked and scarcely any wit," wrote Austen authority John Halperin of Jane's outlook on the society of Bath.

Jane was thrilled to be back in the countryside for the Christmastide season. She and Cassandra alternated between what was now their brother's home, Steventon, and Kent. And then Steventon and Oakley Hall, the home of the Bramstons, and so forth. They arrived in late November at Manydown, home of the Bigg sisters, with the intention of staying through St. Nicholas Day, December 6th.

It was not unusual for Jane and Cassy to be traveling during the holiday season. In previous winters they had spent the holiday at Godmersham, for example, with their wealthy brother Edward Austen Knight.

Godmersham is a village and large civil parish in the Ashford District of Kent, England. The village straddles the Great Stour river. The civil parish includes Godmersham village itself, and Bilting. It shares many of its activities with the neighboring Crundale, a smaller parish to the east.

Godmersham Park House was built in 1732. It is generally thought that Jane's novel *Mansfield Park* was set at Godmersham. "The house, airy and spacious, was made for guests. It was maintained by dozens of servants. Fires were lit in all the bedrooms; breakfast was at ten, dinner might be as late at six thirty; trays of food and drink would be brought to suit everyone's appetite in the hours between," wrote Tomalin.

Edward had been adopted by a wealthy, childless uncle: George's brother Thomas Knight. He was presented to Thomas and his wife Catherine at age twelve. This was not the kind of adoption we think of today; it was a custom in those days when a great estate, title, or fortune was to be handed over.

Edward Austen Knight

Edward remained part of the Austen clan, but he assumed a higher status now with a legitimate title and fortune. This was considered a very fortunate opportunity for Edward.

George Austen's brother, Thomas, had given Rev. Austen the living quarters at Steventon in 1761. Edward was adopted by Thomas and Catherine and became their legal heir in 1783. When Edward turned eighteen, the Knights sent him on a Grand Tour of the continent.

Thomas died in 1794 and left the Godmersham estate to his wife, but she departed Godmersham before her death, moving to Canterbury, at which time Edward accepted

Godmersham Park, Kent, by John Preston Neale, 1824

rightful possession. In 1812 Edward changed his legal name to Knight.

Edward inherited three estates: Steventon, Chawton and Godmersham (which included a manor at Wittersham). Jane loved the libraries at these estates and they were the basis of her education.

The most frequent visitors at Godmersham were the sisters of Elizabeth, Edward's wife. But Jane and Cassy were invited often. Henry also went as often as he could, usually without his scandalous wife, Eliza, even after their marriage.

To many he appeared almost a bachelor uncle, often visiting family alone.

"To Jane, Godmersham was like a dream of elegant living," wrote David Nokes. "Jane found nothing that did not fill her with a kind of wistful longing."

"At Godmersham the rituals of the year were kept with ceremony," wrote Tomalin. "Christmas was celebrated with carols, card games, blind man's bluff, battledore, bullet pudding and dancing; at Twelfth Night there was another feast, and a choosing of a King and Queen from among the children."

Now, in 1802, Jane and Cassy were on the road again for the holidays.

"Jane and Cassy were invited by the Bigg sisters for a stay of several weeks at Manydown, where they had so often enjoyed themselves. Alethea and Catherine were both still single, and Elizabeth Heathcote had come home to her father's house with her baby son William after the tragic early death of her husband that spring," wrote Tomalin.

"The name of Manydown is derived from Many Downs or Manor Down, as it is close to the rolling uplands of southern England," wrote journalist Robert Brown in the *Basingstoke Gazette*. "At the time of the Domesday Survey in 1086, the land was known as Wootton Manor, and was 'held by the prior and convent of St. Swithin.' It remained in their possession until the Dissolution of the Monasteries (1539). In 1338, it is recorded that at Manydown estate (renamed from Wootton Manor) the workers, such as ploughmen and shepherds, received four shillings (now 20 pence) per year. Other documents relate that the dean and chapter of Winchester sold the manor to William Wither, whose family had been farming the land since the early 15th century. But then, in 1660, the dean and chapter decided to reclaim their rights to the land, and the Wither family received no compensation. It took two centuries and the Rev. Lovelace Bigg-Wither to get it back," concluded Brown.

The Bigg family had arrived in Hampshire in 1789. "Widower Lovelace Bigg inherited the mansion from cousins Wither, and hence Mr. Bigg and his two sons changed their names to 'Bigg-Wither.' Three of his five daughters . . . somehow retained the 'Bigg' name," explained the popular and well-regarded Austen fan site BecomingJane.

Manydown had been the scene of one of Jane's tete-a-tetes with Thomas Lefroy. It was where the two starry-eyed youths had been at their most 'shocking.' For Jane, the season of 1802 would be less romantic, but surprisingly exciting all the same. Manydown House was a big, roomy country house, with plenty of space for guests and the staff to serve them. It was only a few miles from Steventon, but to the girls seemed a world away.

The Bigg sisters "were among the best and most affectionate of her friends, and she had known and enjoyed visiting the handsome Manydown house . . . since her girlhood," wrote biographer Joan Rees.

"The five young women had much to talk about and were planning long, cozy winter evenings together; the Bigg sisters may have had something else on their mind as well," wrote Tomalin.

Jane was a few weeks shy of her 27th birthday that Christmas. In her own mind, she and Cassy (who was even older) were staring out into the impending void of spinsterhood. They were both quite aware of their age and its significance.

The Christmastide of 1797, just a few years earlier, had brought Jane's thoughts to bear on marriage once again.

"Jane found herself receiving the attentions of another self-styled suitor. For this she had to thank Madam Lefroy at Ashe. Though she would never admit to it in so many words, Anne Lefroy had felt qualms of conscience at the way she had so abruptly terminated the friendship between Jane Austen and her nephew Tom," wrote Nokes. "As a kind of reparation, she felt it her duty to provide Jane with a more suitable replacement, and at Christmas she invited the Reverend Samuel Blackall, a tall, erudite fellow of Emmanuel College, Cambridge, to stay with her at Ashe. Soon the Reverend Blackall was paying his visits to the Steventon Rectory, where he was entertained by Jane playing the pianoforte pieces she had practiced . . . He, in turn, sought to impress the Austen ladies with lengthy homilies . . . from the virtue of Christian piety to the virtues of green tea and cold veal pies," concluded Nokes.

One instantly sees where Jane might have drawn on moments spent with her brother James and Mr. Blackall, during the comical moment in *Pride and Prejudice* when Mr. Collins bores the Bennet girls to tears by reading the Fordyce's sermons. Blackall's visit that Christmas was brief, and Madam Lefroy entreated the parson to return the next Christmas.

"It would give me particular pleasure to have an opportunity of improving my acquaintance with that family—with the hope of creating to myself a nearer interest. But at present I cannot indulge any expectation of it," Rev. Blackall wrote back to the matchmaking follies of Madam Lefroy.

"This is rational enough," Jane wrote to Cassandra, referencing the Reverend's response, "there is less love and more sense in it than sometimes appeared before, and I am very well satisfied. It will all go on exceedingly well, and decline away in a very reasonable manner."

"The appeal of the noisily perfect Mr. Blackall was the opportunity for private sisterly jokes," commented Nokes.

"There seems no likelihood of his coming to Hampshire this Christmas, and it is therefore most probable that our indifference will soon be mutual," Jane wrote to Cassandra.

Now at Manydown, the season was about to begin, but the festive mood had already started. In residence was Alethea and Catherine's father, Mr. Bigg-Wither, "a hale sixty-year-old; so was their younger brother Harris, who had reached his majority in May. He had been away finishing his education at Worcester College, Oxford, so Jane and Cassandra had not seen him for some time; the shy, stammering boy, although still awkward in manner, had turned into a broad-shouldered, tall and much more confident young man. He was after all the heir to considerable estates," wrote Tomalin.

"Tall, clumsy, and awkward, [Harris Bigg-Wither] would shamble through the house, or lounge on a sofa adding little to the general conversation," wrote Nokes. "His presence would cast something like a blight over the high spirits of his sisters. It was not just his stutter that made him taciturn; he was silent by nature and avoided much society. Brought up as a younger son with six elder sisters, he was accustomed to amuse himself by tormenting his sisters with boyish pranks."

Jane wrote of his gait, that he had a "bad habit of body."

Her perception of Bigg-Withers was no doubt formed and crystalized during the many parlor games that she and her friends played. Card games were always popular, particularly Brag and Speculation.

Brag is a sixteenth century British card game. Players are each dealt three facedown cards. A single round of betting ensues. Each player either places a bet to proceed, or folds. Each player must ante up the same bet played by the first player. The betting continues until only two players remain. At that point, either player in their turn may double the bet, before asking to see his opponent's hand. Then the two hands are revealed. The better hand takes the pot.

Speculation is a simple gambling card game that was popular in the late 18th century and early 19th century. It was popular with Jane Austen and later with Charles Dickens. In Speculation, the dealer sets the ante. Each player antes up. The dealer deals three facedown cards. The dealer then places one face-up card on the table. This is the trump card. The goal of the game is to possess the highest-ranking trump card once all cards left in play have been revealed. Then one by one, each player, in turn, reveals one card. The highest trump card calls the bet for the next round. Each remaining player then turns one more card face up and antes again to stay in the game. Players may fold. Again, the winner calls the next round of betting. This goes on until all cards are revealed. The highest ranking card wins. If the original trump card is not trumped, the pot remains, and the players deal another hand, continuing the betting until the pot is won. If the dealer places an Ace face up as the first card, he wins automatically.

"The preference of Brag over Speculation does not greatly surprise me, I believe, because I feel the same myself," wrote Jane in a letter to Cassandra. "But it mortifies me deeply, because Speculation was under my patronage; and, after all, what is there so delightful in a pair royal of Braggers? It is but three nines or three knaves, or a mixture of them. When one comes to reason upon it, it cannot stand its ground against Speculation—of which I hope Edward is now convinced. Give my love to him if he is," she concluded.

That same Christmastide, Jane passed along this verse to Cassandra to be passed along to her brother:

> Alas! poor Brag, thou boastful game!
> What now avails thine empty name?
> Where now thy more distinguished fame?
> My day is o'er, and thine the same,
> For thou, like me, art thrown aside

At Godmersham, this Christmastide;
And now across the table wide
Each game save brag or spec. is tried.
Such is the mild ejaculation
Of tender-hearted speculation.

Another favorite game among Jane and her family and friends was Bullet Pudding. In the letter below, Fanny Knight, Jane Austen's niece, wrote about their playing at Godmersham Park during a previous Christmas.

Godmersham Park, January 17th 1804

…I was surprised to hear that you did not know what a Bullet Pudding is, but as you don't I will endeavor to describe it as follows:

You must have a large pewter dish filled with flour which you must pile up into a sort of pudding with a peek at top. You must then lay a bullet at top and everybody cuts a slice of it, and the person that is cutting it when it falls must poke about with their noses and chins till they find it and then take it out with their mouths of which makes them strange figures all covered with flour but the worst is that you must not laugh for fear of the flour getting up your nose and mouth and choking you: You must not use your hands in taking the Bullet out.

Snap-dragon was also a popular amusement. "It was another parlor game, but one specifically played in winter in the dark, for it involved picking raisins and almonds out of a punch bowl of flaming spirits, usually brandy," wrote Austen authority J. F. Wakefield. "The blue flame of the lit brandy would have looked spectacular in a darkened room, very similar to effect produced by the tradition of flaming the Christmas Pudding with brandy. In his *Dictionary of the Vulgar Tongue* (1811) Francis Gosse defined the game as follows:

Christmas gambol: raisins and almonds being put into a bowl of brandy, and the candles extinguished, the spirit is set on fire, and the company scramble for the raisins.

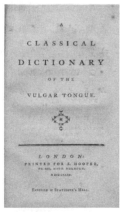

Classical Dictionary of the Vulgar Tongue

"Though brandy does not burn at a particularly high heat it was still possible to be scorched and the point of the fun was to watch peoples' expressions as they darted their fingers through the flames, picking out the fruit or nuts," concluded Wakefield.

Charades was another favorite among the Austens. It was very popular at Steventon and Godmersham, and later at Chawton. There is no reason to think it was not played at other great houses as well.

"In 1895, there appeared an anonymous and private booklet of the charades: and theatrical conundrums written by the Austen family for their own entertainment," wrote Austen and Regency traditions expert Maria Hubert. "The game was played one of two ways. First, it could be a relaxed parlour game, whereby everyone could stay seated. Each player in turn would recite their conundrum, and the rest had to guess at the word. Alternatively, the party would divide into two or more groups, and having decided on their word, they would create short one minute acts to describe the syllables, the last describing the whole word. The word had to be said in the act."

Here are several from the book thought to be by Jane Austen herself:

III
In confinement I'm chained every day
Yet my enemies need not be crowing
To my chain I have always a key,

And no prison can keep me from going.

Small and weak are my hands I'll allow,
Yet for striking my character's great,
Though ruined by one fatal blow
My strokes, if hard pressed, I repeat.

I have neither mouth, eye nor ear
Yet I always keep time as I sing,
Change of season I never need fear,
Though my being depends on the spring.
Would you wish, If these hints are too few ,
One glimpse of my figure to catch?
Look round! I shall soon be in view
If you have but your eyes on the watch.
Answer

IV
Though low is my station
The Chief of the Nation
On me for support oft depend;
Young and old, strong and weak,
My assistance all seek,
Yet all turn their backs on their friend.

At the first rout in town
Every Duchess will own,
My company not a disgrace;
Yet at each rout you'll find
I am still left behind,
And to everyone forced to give place
Without bribe or treat,
I have always a seat
In the Chapel so famed, of St Stephen;
There I lean to no side,
With no party divide, But keep myself steady and even.
Each debate I attend,
From beginning to end,
Yet I seem neither weary nor weaker;
In the house every day Not a word do I say,
Yet in me you behold a good Speaker.
Answer

XV111
When my first is a task to a young girl of spirit,
And my second confines her to finish the piece,
How hard is her fate! But how great is her merit,
If by taking my all she effects her release!
Answer

XIX

Divided, I'm a gentleman public deeds and powers;
United I'm a monster, who
That gentleman devours.
Answer

XX

You may lie on my first by the side of a stream,
And my second compose to the nymph you adore,
But if, when you've none of my whole, her esteem
And affection diminish - think of her no more!
Answer

On the other hand, a child's Christmas in this period was altogether different. For example, at Godmersham, "the children had the usual Christmas dancing and games, Hunt the Slipper, Oranges and Lemons, Wind the Jack, Lighting a Candle in Haste, and Spare Old Noll," wrote Claire Tomalin.

Oranges and Lemons was based on the song of the same name, seemingly published for the first time in *Tommy Thumb's Pretty Song Book* (c. 1744):

Two Sticks and Apple,
  Ring ye Bells at Whitechapple,

Old Father Bald Pate,
  Ring ye Bells Aldgate,
Maids in White Aprons,
  Ring ye Bells at St. Catherines,
Oranges and Lemmons,
  Ring ye bells at St. Clemens,
When will you pay me,
  Ring ye Bells at ye Old Bailey,
When I am Rich,
  Ring ye Bells at Fleetditch,
When will that be,
  Ring ye Bells at Stepney,
When I am Old,
  Ring ye Bells at Pauls.

"There is considerable variation in the churches and lines attached to them in versions printed in the late eighteenth and early nineteenth centuries," wrote Austen scholar Laura Boyle. "Two children form an arch with their arms. They determine in secret which of them shall be an 'orange' and which a 'lemon.' Everyone sings the 'Oranges and Lemons' song. The other children in the game take turns to run under the arch until one of them is caught when the arch falls at the end of the song. The captured player is asked privately whether they will be an 'orange' or a 'lemon' and then goes behind the original 'orange' or 'lemon' team leader. The game and singing then starts over again. At the end of the game there is usually 'a tug of war' to test whether the 'oranges' or 'lemons' are stronger."

But another parlor game was afoot, on December 2nd, 1802.

"Jane was no doubt very fond of her friend's brother, whom she would have danced with as a child," wrote Tomalin.

The Bigg-Wither family were warm and welcoming, pleased to have the Austen sisters with them again. Jane and Cassandra were so much at ease and off their guard that neither noticed that the twenty-one year-old Harris was being particularly attentive and that Jane was responding to him with comfortable familiarity," wrote Jon Spence.

On the evening of December 2nd, after Jane and Cassandra had been at Manydown only a week, Harris, in the library or perhaps the drawing room, and shocked Jane with a proposal of marriage.

"I can give the exact date of Mr. Wither's proposal to my Aunt from pocket-book entries which make no allusion to anything of the sort—but some peculiar coming and goings coinciding exactly with what my Mother more than once told me of that affair, leave me no doubt that the offer was made, & accepted at Manydown on Thursday the 2nd of December, 1802," wrote Jane's niece Caroline, daughter of Mary and James, who were at that time ensconced at Steventon.

Harris Bigg-Wither

"His evident affection for her was something she had never expected; and was certainly very flattering. 'It is something for a woman to be assured, in her eight-and-twenty year, that she has not lost the charm of her earlier youth,'" wrote Nokes.

"It cannot be known whether Jane was unprepared for his proposal and accepted it out of surprise and embarrassment, or whether she had recognized he was gathering courage to make it," wrote Rees.

As Tomalin posited, it had been seven years since Jane had flirted so openly with Tom Lefroy in this very house. "She had let the world see it, not minding if she were talked about. It was even possible that Harris had kept a vision of Jane as she had been then, dancing so recklessly and happily."

"For all her rationality, Jane Austen was an impulsive woman. She had come to adore Eliza after only a few days; she had fallen in love with Tom the first time they met and made no attempt to conceal it. This time it was not to an individual Jane responded to; it was to all that Harris signified," wrote Spence.

Jane's friends and family agreed that she should marry him. "Materially at least this would have been a good match for her," wrote biographer Halperin. "Her father had little money to leave her; Harris was in a position to help him in his last years. The lot of a penurious spinster was of course not a happy one."

"In the circumstances, it might almost be argued that it would be a piece of recklessness not to marry him," wrote Nokes.

Jane echoes this sentiment in *The Watsons*: "You know we must marry," Miss Watson reminds her younger sister Emma. "I could do very well single for my own part. A little company, and a pleasant ball now and then, would be enough for me, if one could be young forever; but my father cannot provide for us, and it is very bad to grow old and be poor and laughed at."

Like Miss, Watson, Jane accepted. "No doubt the family were told the happy news, Harris's father and sisters were delighted, and Jane departed to bed amid universal rejoicing," considered Rees.

Surely there was wine and toasts and congratulations, and the hope of a very special Christmastide that year.

"On the face of it, her acceptance was natural and sensible," wrote Joan Rees. Jane loved the Bigg-Wither girls. Harris was heir to a good fortune and lands. And she had always regarded Manydown as a home away from home. Rees continued:

> For a woman in Jane Austen's financial position, the opportunity of marriage, motherhood, and eventually becoming the mistress of such an establishment, where one day she might be able to offer her sister a comfortable home, was not an offer to be turned down lightly.
>
> To be removed from a situation of relative poverty in rented lodgings in Bath and to be transformed into the mistress of such a magnificent estate as Manydown; an estate, moreover, within in a few miles of the scenes of her childhood, surrounded by family and friends. This was an opportunity which she might well have believed to exceed her wildest aspirations.

But in her bed that night, Jane replayed the events of the day. Her head was spinning. What had she done? She loved Manydown, and Alethea and Catherine, but she did not love Harris.

"The night went by, and Jane stayed awake, like a heroine in a novel who cannot sleep because too many emotions are pressing in on her: 'the sleepless couch, which is the true heroine's portion . . . a pillow strewn with thorns and wet with tears,' as she had written mockingly about herself," wrote Tomalin.

"Presumably a night of agonized reflection had brought home the enormity of what she had done," wrote Mac-Donagh. Frightening "pictures of married life with Harris which sprang to mind, as she thought through the actualities, during the course of her internal debate."

One can only imagine Jane, in her bedroom at Many-down, tossing and turning in bed. She might finally have gotten up and lit a candle, pacing the floor, or simply looking out a dark window in the dead of night, or watching the first light begin to break in the early morning hours.

"The sleepless night dragged by; in the battleground of Jane's heart and mind, sense was totally defeated by sensibility. She did not love Harris and she could not marry him," wrote Rees. "Harris himself had clearly failed to make an impression on Jane, however much she herself had succeeded in attracting him."

Surely, to be related to the sisters she so very much adored would be lovely, but the thought of being betrothed to this young man seemed very overwhelming.

"She was fond of him as the brother of her friends; she yearned for the security he offered; but she did not want to be married to him," wrote Spence.

"She thought and thought; and in the morning she packed her bag, dressed herself grimy, and sought someone—Alethea perhaps—who would find Harris. Again they were closeted alone in the library, or the small drawing room, and this time Jane explained, with all the delicacy in her power, that she had made a mistake and could not after all marry him. She esteemed him, she was honored by his proposal, but on thinking it over she realized that esteem and respect were not enough, and that she would not be behaving fairly or rightly towards him if she accepted the offer of his hand," wrote Tomalin.

One can only imagine the impending disaster about to take place in the hallways of that great house that morning. While Jane's bedroom had been filled with angst and tension, the young man in question and his parents, his sisters, and Cassandra had all slept well, thinking a new match, and yet another chord of affection, would soon be in place between the two families. While Jane spent the night in dread, the rest of the house woke to a happy and beautiful new morning filled with promise and affection. All of it about to be crushed.

"Whether or not he was truly in love with her, Harris's hopes had been dashed from joy to dismay overnight. Miserable and hurt, he may have also felt he had been made to look ridiculous. The rest of the family was sorry for Harris, and surprised and disappointed by Jane's sudden and determined change of mind," wrote Rees.

"To be sure, she should not have said 'Yes' overnight; but I have always respected her courage in cancelling that 'Yes' the next morning; all worldly advantages would have been to her, and she was of an age to know this quite well," wrote Jane's niece Caroline, many years later. "My aunts had very small fortunes; and on their father's death, they and their mother would be, they were aware, but poorly off. I believe most young women so circumstanced would have gone on trusting to love after marriage."

Certainly the revulsion must have been powerful for Jane Austen to have committed such a faux-pas as to jilt Bigg-Wither out of hand after accepting him just the night before—and with such gaiety. "Her courage in facing him, and 'explaining herself' in person to him so quickly, might be applauded later on. But at the moment of the rupture it must have seemed to his family an aggravation of the slight, and to hers evidence of want of consideration and responsibility towards the Austen men on whom she depended for her support," reasoned MacDonagh.

Certainly Jane would relive this anguish and share her fears when she wrote about Charlotte marrying the Reverend Collins in *Pride and Prejudice*.

"Jane Austen could not, it appears, play the role of Charlotte Luca—twenty-seven when she accepts Mr. Collins—after all; she could not, that is, marry a man she didn't love simply in order to have an establishment of her own," wrote Halperin.

"A marital engagement was a contract between families. No matter how bizarre or mute the scene at Manydown's entrance-hall was it involved more than a few people," added Haleprin. "Servants certainly rushed to and fro with belongings, people appeared and vanished, a carriage rolled up and was not occupied. Eyes tried to speak, trembling embraces were repeated. And suddenly two young ladies were a moving under a blur of trees."

To add insult to injury, the girls did not own their own carriage, so the Bigg-Wither family had to chauffer Jane and Cassandra in one of the family's carriages back to Steventon. An awkward journey to be sure, that morning.

Jane wept openly. Cassandra was vexed, but defended her to their unhappy sister-in-law, Mary, who had not expected the girls for quite some time yet. Mary was not sympathetic. It had been a good proposal, in her estimation. A good match. Now, Jane and Cassandra would inconvenience the family and her brother considerably. They insisted James take them back to their lodgings in Bath immediately. This upset Mary even more.

Walking the semi-deserted streets of Bath that Christmas, the wounds still fresh, Jane pondered what she had done. "She had much to pay for and could not quickly set things right . . . she had repaid hospitality with adventurousness," wrote Honan. "In a moment of carelessness she had struck through Harris at Alethea and Catherine, who could hardly fail to feel upset. Very, very little that she could tell the Biggs girls could quickly absolve her of the guilt of misleading them, of imagining and playing with notions of what would be best for Harris, herself, her parents . . . it was only in the aftermath of reflection that she plumbed the depths of what constituted 'sense.' One of her sources in novel writing was clearly the reconstruction of moods, feelings and perceptions after she had seen the folly of them, and it is unmistakably true that she had more than a few blunders to draw upon."

Several years later, Harris would meet a young woman who was in love with him named Anne Howe Frith. They eventually married, and though time healed Harris's wounds, scars remained.

But that Christmastide, the women spent the holiday in their rented house in Bath (where they lived somewhat penuriously) with their elderly parents, a somewhat dreary alternative to the country Christmases they knew so well and loved. Two women in their early thirties, at the peak of their physical being, stuck in a small set of rooms in one of England's most fashionable spa towns, isolated and depressed. As the aftermath of the incident began to unwind, and the women shared these quiet and cold days, Jane inevitably returned to her writing.

"The fiasco with Harris seems to have returned her to her manuscripts," wrote Tomalin. "She had been carrying these precious bundles around from place to place, year after year."

According to Tomalin, Jane then began copying out and revising *Susan*, which later became *Northanger Abbey*.

1809

PART FIVE: 1809

In January of 1805, George Austin took ill and suddenly died. The episode was shocking to the family. The remaining women—Jane, Cassandra, and their mother—were forced to move into rented living quarters on Gay Street in Bath, a much less tony area of the city than where they had been living. The girls now depended primarily upon their brothers for support, and lived in a shabbier lifestyle than they had been accustomed to.

Henry was Jane's favorite brother. With her father gone, Henry was never long out of Jane's thoughts. "In 1803 and 1804 Henry and Eliza [had] joined his parents and sisters, who were at that time living in Bath, for holidays at Lyme Regis," wrote Austen expert J. David Grey. At the time of their father's death, Henry was changing careers. It came at a time when Jane, and her mother, and Cassandra required help in the form of money and shelter.

"Just starting in the banking business, Henry contributed £50 a year to their support and claimed he would 'do as much as long as [his] precarious income remains.' Later his mother confessed, in a letter written in 1820 to her sister-in-law Jane Leigh-Perrot, that this amount had been withdrawn by her son after his bankruptcy in 1816," continued Grey. "Henry and two associates had founded a banking institution in London sometime between 1804 and 1806.

Henry Austen

Austen, Maunde and Tilson of Covent Garden flourished and enabled Henry and Eliza to move from Brompton (where Jane Austen had found the quarters cramped during a visit in 1808) to a more fashionable address and larger house at 64 Sloane Street. Jane's visits here in 1811 and 1813 were happy events, filled with parties, theatre-going, and the business of publishing *Sense and Sensibility* and *Pride and Prejudice*."

In October of 1806, all three women moved in with brother Frank in Southampton, who had just married. Frank was now a captain in the Royal Navy. In October 1805, as Captain of HMS Canopus, a French ship of the line captured in the Battle of the Nile (as the Franklin), Austen was temporarily detached from Admiral Nelson's fleet for convoy duty in the Mediterranean. While he missed the opportunity to participate in the Battle of Trafalgar, he did command the Canopus a year later in the Battle of San Domingo.

Less than a year later, in March 1807, they moved to a modest home on Castle Square in Southampton. They lived there a short period later until they received an invitation to move to Chawton House, on October 24th, 1808.

"Henry obligingly looked the house over for them and reported there were six bedrooms and garrets for storage. Mrs. Austen daydreamed of employing a manservant who could sleep in one of the garrets. Jane hoped to be settled at Chawton by the end of the next summer," wrote Austen biographer Valerie Grosvenor Myer.

That Christmas in Southampton had been another in a series of dreary holidays set in their urban environs. Brother James's wife paid them a visit to Castle Square in 1808. James was now worth 1,100 pounds a year, and wealthy enough to afford a carriage and three horses. Their children were being invited to area balls, and as proud parents they could not wait to share the details.

"After their departure on Christmas day, the house at Castle Square seemed strangely quiet. Mrs. F[rank Austen] sent a message for more clothes, which disappointed Jane by its clear implication that she and Frank did not envisage 'a very early return to us.' Snow lay on the ground for more than a week, which was most unusual for Southampton, and the occasional visitors to Castle Square seemed scarcely less frosty," wrote David Nokes.

According to Nokes, "One dull evening was spent 'yawning and shivering' in a silent, lugubrious company, their chairs drawn up in a wide circle around the fire. Only

Chawton House, Hampshire

the widgeon and preserved ginger ('delicious') rescued the evening from being utterly wretched."

As they lingered in Southampton waiting for Chawton House to be readied, Jane alternated between euphoria at the prospect of moving and determination to enjoy the season as much as she could.

"A larger circle of acquaintance, and an increase of amusement, is quite in character with our approaching removal. Yes, I mean to go to as many balls as possible, that I may have a good bargain. Everybody is very much concerned at our going away, and everybody is acquainted with Chawton, and speaks of it as a remarkably pretty village, and everybody knows the house we describe, but nobody fixes on the right," Jane wrote to Cassandra, who was at Godmersham with Henry and Eliza. Cassandra's visit to Godmersham had stretched on for several months, and it was clear Jane longed for her sister's return.

"Our ball was rather more amusing than I expected. Martha liked it very much, and I did not gape till the last quarter of an hour. It was past nine before we were sent for, and not twelve when we returned. The room was tolerably full, and there were, perhaps, thirty couple[s] of dancers. The melancholy part was to see so many dozen young women standing by without partners, and each of them with two ugly naked shoulders," Jane reported that December to Cassandra. "It was the same room in which we danced fifteen years ago. I thought it all over, and in spite of the shame of being so much older, felt with thankfulness that I was quite as happy now as then. We paid an additional shilling for our tea, which we took as we chose in an adjoining and very comfortable room."

It was clearly apparent in the letter to Cassandra that Jane had not lost her lust for the battlefield and gamesmanship that was the ballroom. She wrote, "There were only four dances, and it went to my heart that the Miss Lances (one of them, too, named Emma) should have partners only for two. You will not expect to hear that I was asked to dance, but I was—by the gentleman whom we met that Sunday with Captain D'Auvergne. We have always kept up a bowing acquaintance since, and, being pleased with his black eyes, I spoke to him at the ball, which brought on me this civility; but I do not know his name, and he seems so little at home in the English language that I believe his black eyes may be the best of him."

"Jane was approaching her thirty-third birthday and according to the standards of the day she was on the shelf," wrote Myer. "Formal introductions no longer seemed indispensable to her. At this stage in her life such attention seemed flattering rather than insulting."

"I am glad you are to have Henry with you again; with him and the boys you cannot but have a cheerful, and at times even a merry, Christmas," concluded Jane towards the end of the letter.

Jane, Cassandra, and Mrs. Austen took up residence at Chawton on July 7th, 1809.

"At Chawton, things would be different. Here, once again, they would be compelled to furnish their own amusements. There could be nothing more suitable for filling long afternoons and evening, when they were neither visiting nor visited, or when the weather was not suitable for walking, or when the mood did not incline to playing her pianoforte, than reading and writing," wrote Nokes.

Looking forward to Chawton, Jane wrote to Cassandra that Christmastide, "Yes, yes, we will have a pianoforte, as good a one as can be got

Illustration of the pianoforte by C. E. Brock, from the 1895 edition of Pride and Prejudice

for thirty guineas, and I will practise country dances, that we may have some amusement for our nephews and nieces, when we have the pleasure of their company."

"Jane Austen's writing falls into two distinct phases, Steventon and Chawton, before and after the unhappy period in Bath," wrote Myer. "The early burlesques, *Catharine*, or *The Bower*, and the original drafts of her early novels were written at Steventon before the move to Bath in 1800 . . . Soon after the move to Chawton in 1809, the second fertile period began. Jane started revising her earlier novels for the press."

Chawton is a village and civil parish in the East Hampshire district of Hampshire, England. The village lies within the South Downs National Park. Chawton's recorded history dates back to the Domesday survey of 1086. The owner, John St. John, served as deputy to Edward I in Scotland. Henry III visited the Elizabethan manor house on more than forty occasions. The village of Chawton has a single church, St Nicholas, which has stood on the site since at least 1270.

Chawton Cottage is a roomy and unpretentious home in the village. It had ample bedrooms, a kitchen, a bake house, and was sparely, but elegantly decorated in the style of the day.

"The house was L-shaped, of old red brick, at least a hundred years old, and probably built as a posting inn; there were two main stories, and attics above under the tiled roof," described Tomalin.

"The first real room you enter is the drawing-room, one of the two 'parlours' that the Austen ladies had. The new Gothic window gave them a view over the garden, which was set to the side of the house, and the Winchester Road which bordered the garden was screened by a high wooden fence to give them more privacy from prying eyes in coaches travelling to Winchester and beyond," wrote Austen authority J.M. Wakefield.

Jane was so taken with their new home that she wrote to her brother Francis on July 26th, 1809:

> . . . as for ourselves, we're very well,
> As unaffected prose will tell.
> Cassandra's pen will give our state
> The many comforts that await
> Our Chawton Home - how much we find
> Already in it to our mind,
> And how convinced that when complete,
> It will all other houses beat,
> That ever have been made or mended,
> With rooms concise or rooms distended.
> You'll find us very snug next year . . .

Brother Edward arrived at Chawton on October 21st, 1809, with Fanny and his fifth son, Charles. They stayed until the second week of November. At Christmastide 1809, the Austen women would have brought greenery indoors. The mantles and windows would be sparsely but carefully decorated.

"In spring and summer they have simple small posies of flowers from the garden on show but at this time of the year . . . the Austen ladies may have done for Christmas, in common with many other Georgian families . . . the drawing-room fireplace is decked with boughs of evergreens, ivy and yew, and some oranges studded with cloves have been added (though the Austen ladies may have preferred not to use oranges this way but to make their store of expensive oranges into wine . . .)," observed Wakefield.

This was an incredibly happy period in Jane's life. The family was relatively secure and back in the country, where the customs and pace of life were in keeping with the days of their childhood; they had a richer, more familiar hue.

"The cottage stands at the end of a very quiet street," wrote biographer Park Honan. "Jane Austen could wake up in a green setting to see tilled fields, a pond, and groves of ash and elm from a front window. When it rained, her mother kept the curtains opened."

Jane immersed herself in a sheltered country lifestyle. According to Sarah Woolsey, an archivist of Austen's correspondence:

Miss Austen's life coincided with two of the momentous epochs of history—the American struggle for independence, and the French Revolution; but there is scarcely an allusion to either in her letters. She was interested in the fleet and its victories because two of her brothers were in the navy and had promotion and prize-money to look forward to. In this connection she mentions Trafalgar and the Egyptian expedition, and generously remarks that she would read Southey's "Life of Nelson" if there was anything in it about her brother Frank. Further than that, the making of the gooseberry jam and a good recipe for orange wine interests her more than all the marchings and counter-marchings, the manoeuvers and diplomacies, going on the world over. In the midst of the universal vortex of fear and hope, triumph and defeat, while the fate of Britain and British liberty hung trembling in the balance, she sits writing her letters, trimming her caps, and discussing small beer with her sister in a lively and unruffled fashion wonderful to contemplate.

"The society of rural England in those days," as British journalist and historian Goldwin Smith put it, "enjoyed a calm of its own in the midst of the European tempest like the windless center of a circular storm."

Jane and her family had long made special brews for this time of year. "The Austens were enthusiastic home brewers, bottling their own wines, beers, and of course, Mead," wrote Austen authority Laura Boyle.

In December of 1808, Jane wrote in a letter to Cassandra at Godmersham Park, "It is you, however, in this instance, that have the little children, and I that have the great cask, for we are brewing spruce beer again; but my meaning really is, that I am extremely foolish in writing all this unnecessary stuff when I have so many matters to write about that my paper will hardly hold it all. Little matters they are, to be sure, but highly important."

Jane was not above imbibing, especially during the Christmastide season. She once wrote to Cassandra, "I should inevitably fall a sacrifice to the arts of some fat woman who would make me drunk with small beer."

Spruce beer was a popular favorite during this period. Recipes might be shared amongst neighbors, and men returning from the British armed forces, whether on land or from sea, had picked up the recipes as part of regulations.

While in their majestey's service, many had acquired a taste for spruce beer. Orders for the Highland Regiment in North America, in June of 1759, stipulated that "Spruce beer is to be brewed for the health and convenience of the troops which will be served at prime cost. Five quarts of molasses will be put into every barrel of Spruce beer. Each gallon will cost nearly three coppers."

"Winter orders that year instructed that each post should keep enough molasses on hand to make two quarts of beer for each man every day. Whether it was brewed for health, holiday drinking, or simply as a tasty alternative to water (that's debatable), Spruce beer was a common drink in Georgian England. Brewed along similar lines as Root Beer and Ginger Beer, it could be drunk fresh or allowed to ferment," wrote Austen authority Laura Boyle.

According to home brewing authority David Ackley, "Trees and their branches, barks, and berries have been used traditionally for flavoring beers, especially in Scandinavian countries, for hundreds of years. Juniper, spruce, and fir are some of the most common . . . In North America, spruce beer was used by American colonists to prevent scurvy. For the adventurous forager, spruce can be found in the evergreen forests of North America. Cuttings from new growth are best for brewing. Make a tea by boiling the branches in water for 30 minutes. Strain out the branches and add this homemade spruce essence to your mash or boil."

From American Cookery: Or the Art of Dressing Viands, Fish, Poultry and Vegetables, *by Amelia Simmons, 1796:*

For brewing Spruce beer. Take four ounces of hops, let them boil half an hour, in one gallon of water, strain the hop water, then add 16 gallons of warm water, two gallons of molasses, eight ounces of essence of spruce, dissolved in one quart of water, put it in a clean cask, then shake it well together, add half a pint of emptins [baker's yeast], then let it stand and work one week, if very warm weather less time will do, when it is drawn off to bottle, add one spoonful of molasses to every bottle.

Sparkling with a taste somewhat near dry champagne, Ginger beer was possibly the most popular small beer in England at that time. "Originating in England in the mid 1700's, by 1790, the recipe had crossed the Atlantic, though significant portion of the American Ginger beer was still imported by ship from England. One of the reasons that England could export Ginger beer was because of the quality of the stoneware bottles it was stored in. In 1835, England developed a superior glazing process called Improved Bristol Glaze. After filling, these bottles were corked and wired to maintain the pressure. This kept the alcohol and carbon dioxide in solution, both of which acted as preservatives, allowing for a long shelf life," wrote Laura Boyle.

Ginger Beer Recipe
by Martha Lloyd, dear friend of Jane Austen

Two gallons of water, two oz. Cream of Tartar. Two lbs of lump sugar. Two lemons sliced, 2 oz. of ginger bruised. Pour the water boiling on the ingredients, then add two spoonfuls of good yeast; when cold bottle it in stone bottles, tie down the corks. It is fit to drink in 48 hours—a little more sugar is an improvement; glass bottles would not do.

The Austens also made wine. Jane was the keeper of tea, wine, beer, and other spirits. She had once written to Cassandra, many years earlier, "Yesterday I had the agreeable surprise of finding several scarlet strawberries quite ripe; had you been at home, this would have been a pleasure lost. There are more gooseberries and fewer currants than I thought at first. We must buy currants for our wine." Jane liked her wine, and wrote in another letter to her sister, "I am put on the sofa near the fire, and can drink as much wine as I like."

Mead was another favorite with the Austens. Jane once wrote to Cassandra, "Oh, thank you very much for your long letter; it did me a great deal of good. Henry accepts your offer of making his nine gallons of mead thankfully."

Mead is an alcoholic beverage created by fermenting honey and water. It can be made plain as well as flavored with various fruits, spices, grains or hops. (Hops act as a preservative and produce a bitter, beer-like flavor.) The alcoholic content of mead may range from about 8% ABV to more than 20%. Mead may be still, carbonated, or naturally sparkling. It also comes in all manner of tastes: dry, semisweet, or sweet. Mead is among man's oldest potables, dating as far back as 1700 BC. Well-established in England by 700 AD, it was a very common drink in rural areas.

"It can be regarded as the ancestor of all fermented drinks," food historian Maguelonne Toussaint-Samat has speculated, "antedating the cultivation of the soil." In the opinion of Claude Lévi-Strauss, mead marked the passage of man "from nature to culture."

Jane wrote of mead again many years later to Cassandra, "We hear now that there is to be no honey this year. Bad news for us. We must husband our present stock of mead, and I am sorry to perceive that our twenty gallons is very nearly out. I cannot comprehend how the fourteen gallons could last so long."

Jane Austen's dear friend Martha Lloyd kept a book full of recipes used in the Austen household. Among them is the Austen Mead recipe, which Jane loved so well that she wrote, in 1813, from Godmersham, "I find time in the midst of Port & Mediera to think of the 14 bottles of mead very often . . . "

To Make Mead

To every gallon of water put 4 lbs of honey, and for 20 gallons add as follows: 2 oz of nutmeg, half an oz of mace, half an oz of cloves, 2 ozs of race-ginger, all just bruised, and sewed up in a linene bag; then add a large handful of sweet briar with the above, boil it all together for an hour, skimming it all the time it boils; then drain it off. Add a little balm to it, if it does not work, turn it and let it stand a day or two. Then add the juice of 6 good lemons, with the rind of them and your bag of spices in the barrel. Stop it up close for 10 or 12 months. Then bottle it for use. You may add some more spices if you like it.

To entertain company properly, especially during the Christmastide season, the ladies at Chawton needed some potent potables for their gentlemen guests as well as something for the ladies. Punches were another excellent way to serve something fun and different. Since punches were often flavored with fruits, and sweetened, these drinks were more appealing to visiting ladies. Ladies and gentlemen of their era prided themselves on their individual concoctions and exchanged recipes frequently.

"The Georgian era is widely known for its excesses, the least of which was heavy drinking. A typical Georgian gentleman of leisure would spend his days frequenting one of the myriad coffee rooms and his evenings, many times into the wee hours, in a gaming house, tavern, or gentleman's club roistering with his cronies over a brimming punch bowl," wrote food historian Emory Lee.

"Punch began as a sailors' drink, where everyone onboard—officers and ordinary seamen alike—would partake together. It didn't always exercise that equalizing force, but it's inherent in the format. A bowl of punch is a group effort, and people who choose not to partake find themselves at odds with the community. Most will put aside their standoffish ways and join in, but if they can't or won't, the nice thing is that nobody cares: all the more punch for us," offered spirits and cocktails historian David Wondrich.

The word 'punch' is an adaptation of the Hindi word 'paantsch,' which means 'five,' because the mixture was usually based on a recipe blending five ingredients: spirits, sugar, lemon, water, and tea (or spices). Punch was brought back to England by sailors of the British East India Company in the early seventeenth century, and spread throughout Europe from there. Ornate punch bowls—ceramic or silver—quickly became popular. This was a time before bottling had become commonplace. It was the easiest way to serve guests, and it was thought to be fun and festive.

"Punch was phenomenally popular during the long 18th century. It developed as a drink as a result of the opening up of trade between Europe and the Far East," wrote Wakefield.

"Christmas parties aren't what they used to be. Take the one British Admiral Edward Russell threw in Cádiz in 1694 for the sailors of his fleet and their Spanish hosts: 6,000 guests, 150 dishes (including a whole roast ox), and in the center, a tiled fountain full of punch and a ship's boy floating in the middle in a little rowboat ladling out the punch," wrote David Wondrich. "Admiral Russell's punch was first served on Christmas Day, 1694, and is delicious, although you might want to make less than the original 1200 gallons, unless you're expecting a lot of people."

Admiral Russell's Punch
from Punch *by David Wondrich*

Servings: 12 to 18

6 lemons

1 cup raw sugar

1 750-ml bottle VSOP-grade Cognac

1 cup lightly sweet oloroso or amontillado Sherry (such as Dry Sack 15-year-old or Sandeman Character)

Freshly grated nutmeg

1. Fill 4-cup metal bowl with water. Freeze overnight (for ice mold).

2. Remove peels from 4 lemons in strips. Place in medium bowl. Add sugar and muddle. Let stand 30 minutes. Muddle again.

3. Cut peeled and unpeeled lemons in half; juice enough lemons to yield 1 cup juice. Bring 1 cup water to boil in small saucepan; pour over lemon peel mixture and stir until sugar dissolves. Strain syrup into large bowl; discard peels. Mix in lemon juice. Add Cognac, Sherry, and 4 cups cold water. Cover punch and refrigerate until cold, at least 2 hours and up to 6 hours.

*4. Dip ice mold in hot water to release ice block. Turn
ice block, rounded side up, in punch bowl. Add punch.
Sprinkle with nutmeg. Ladle into small cups and serve.*

An even more commonly used recipe was for Royal Punch.
The original recipe for Punch Royal appeared in John Nott's
book, *The Cook's and Confectioner's Dictionary*, published in
London in 1723.

Punch Royal

*Take three pints of the best brandy, as much spring-wa-
ter, a pint or better of the best lime-juice, a pound of
double refined sugar.*

*This punch is better than weaker punch, for it does not
so easily affect the head, by reason of the large quantity
of lime-juice more than common, and is more grateful
and comfortable to the stomach.*

"The taste for drinking punch still remained fashionable,
even if it was not served in a bowl, but in individual glasses.
As a method of conspicuous consumption it still remained
popular," wrote Wakefield. "Punch was an expensive and

time consuming drink to prepare. The rind of citrus fruit had to be carefully removed in a spiral for decorative purposes; the juice of citrus fruit lemons orange or limes had to be squeezed by hand and sieved of its pips through a muslin strainer; the sugar and spices—expensive commodities both—had to be mixed in correct proportions and finally the expensive spirits added. The spiral cut rinds of oranges were traditionally dangled in and over the edge of the bowl."

Something with a bit more fizz, and jut a little less alcohol, was the popular Prince of Wales Punch.

Prince of Wales Punch

Three bottles of Champagne, two of Madeira, one of Hock, one of Curacao, one quart of Brandy, one pint of Rum, and two bottles of seltzer water, flavored with four pounds of bloom raisins, Seville oranges, lemons, white sugar candy and diluted with iced green tea instead of water.

But not all were brewing and bubbling. The everyday life proceeded apace at Chawton. Domestic life had a steady, reliable cadence all its own. There was a routine that was happily attended to, as the home needed to be maintained, meals cooked, gardens tended, etc.

"Between them, Jane and Cassandra determined upon a division of the household duties which their mother was now too elderly to attend to and which might not be entrusted to their maid's care. Jane's own duties were chiefly confined to the mornings. After practicing her music, it was her task to make breakfast at precisely 9 o'clock," wrote Nokes.

"There were always a few servants in the several households Jane Austen occupied, but never so many that the family escaped a share of domestic duties. [Jane] was probably ambivalent about such tasks, taking at least a minor pleasure in what she was obliged to do," wrote novelist Carol Shields.

"Aunt Cassandra did all the rest," said her niece Anna. Thankfully for Jane and Cassandra, they had the help of their friend and companion Martha Lloyd to share in their burdens.

Martha Lloyd lived with the Austen ladies for many years, and eventually married Jane's elder brother. The Lloyds were friends of the Austens and had known each other for many years. Martha was the eldest daughter of Rev. Noyes Lloyd of Bishopstone in Wiltshire, and his wife Martha Craven. In 1789, the Reverend Lloyd passed away. Afterwords, the Lloyd family lived at the parsonage of Deane for approximately two years, through the grace of Reverend George Austen. It was at this time that Martha Lloyd and her sister Mary grew to be affectionate friends of Cassandra and Jane.

"Ever since Mr. Austen's death, it had been privately agreed amongst them all that Martha, who was now quite alone in the world, should come to live with the Austens in Bath," wrote Nokes.

"I am quite of your opinion as to the folly of concealing any longer our intended partnership with Martha," Jane wrote Cassandra, "& whenever there has of late been an enquiry on the subject I have always been sincere."

Martha moved in with the Austen family during their time at Bath, and followed them to Southampton and then to Chawton. Jane considered Martha to be a second sister. "With what true sympathy our feelings are shared by Martha, you need not be told;—she is the friend & Sister under every circumstance," Jane wrote Cassandra on October 13th, 1808, by which time Martha's parents had both passed on. Jane and Cassandra now were her family for all intents and purposes.

Martha took on many duties as housekeeper for the family, though the work was divided among all the women. Martha's role as Jane Austen's friend and confidante cannot be undervalued and her contribution to what we know of Austen's life is significant. We not only have letters written by Jane to Martha, but Martha's collection of recipes used at Chawton as well.

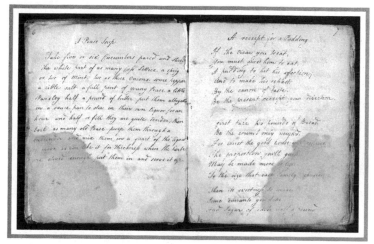

Martha Lloyd's Recipe Book, Jane Austen's House Museum

Martha's hand-written household book, now the property of the Jane Austen Memorial Trust, provides a fascinating picture of domestic life at that time. The day-to-day affairs of the Austens and their circle reflect the general preoccupations of the 'middling people' during that period, especially the pleasures of the table. In the volume she collected, Martha personally curated material from the novelist's letters and books, as well as family recollections, and combined recipes and medicinal hints. The volume illustrates the changes in appetites and the times of meals. It has also helped us to chart cooking innovations from open fires to iron ranges, observe fluctuating food prices, and marvel at the ingenuity of preserving food in special ice houses.

Martha catalogued a wide variety of recipes including cowheel soup, a recipe for Indian curried chicken, a very good orange pudding, fish sauces, and pickled samphire and cowslip wine. There was also a recipe to cure worms or 'hooping cough' and even instructions on how to whiten silk stockings and polish boots.

"Martha Lloyd's recipe book is of course one of the treasures of the museum. Her recipes must have been prepared in [the current kitchen at Chawton]. It's all rather wonderful to think that her recipes and the room are now all in working order . . . food being such an important part of Jane Austen's novels and letters," wrote Wakefield.

"Kitchens . . . were changing and being modernized at this period. Cooking had formerly been done over the open fire in the great fireplaces, with racks to hang pots and kettles, and spits to roast meats," wrote Eileen Sutherland, an Austen enthusiast. "On tables and in odd corners are spice boxes, canisters for tea and coffee, vinegar barrels, mincing and grinding machines, pestles and mortars, vast milk jugs, and brass skimmers. The ceiling was well stored with hanging provisions of various kinds, such as sugar loaves, black puddings, hams, sausages, and flitches of bacon."

While the kitchen was attached to the cottage, the bake house was separate.

"A baking oven was separately fired—usually by building the fire inside the oven itself until it was hot enough, then raking out the ashes, sweeping it clean, and putting in the bread to be baked," wrote Sutherland. "When the bread was finished, a second baking, at a lower temperature, could be done with the reserved heat. Most ordinary homes did not have their own baking ovens," continued Sutherland. "The local baker would usually agree—perhaps for a small fee—to bake the neighbours' dinners after his bread baking was done."

"Just outside the bake house was the well, which was needed to provide copious amounts of water for the laundry, which was done in the Bakehouse too. This is the 'copper': the bricks house a copper container. A fire would be lit underneath and the cottons boiled in the upper compartment, now covered with a wooden lid," wrote J.F. Wakefield. "The baking for the Austen household took place here too and the proximity of the well and the copper made the Bakehouse the perfectly practical place for boiling water . . . "

According to the Jane Austen House Museum, "Late Georgian food was exciting, delicious and a way of displaying identity. Kitchens were a hive of activity: pounding, plucking and debating the merits [of] French vs English cuisine. It was a period when British classics, such as pies, puddings and cakes all came to the fore, but also one in which the aristocracy employed only French cooks, and French food was all the rage."

"My downstairs sitting room was once the Austens' kitchen," wrote former Jane Austen House Museum director, Jean K. Bowden. "When it was being redecorated before I moved in, our architect took the opportunity to find out if there was anything behind the rather horrid modern fireplace. Lo and behold, there was a large inglenook, with two little wooden seats on either side, and a bar above to hang the bacon on to be cured in the smoke from the fire. You could stand inside it and look right up to the stars— no wonder it was bricked up—the downdraught must have been terrible, to say nothing of the rain coming down the chimney! You can still see where the turning of the spit to roast the meat has worn away the brickwork."

One "can imagine Cook, and Sally (with her new red cloak) and Betsy, the maids, and the men-servants Browning (who was good with the dogs) and, later, William (a good-looking young man, according to Jane)—all, at their various times, sitting around the kitchen fire, or, more probably, working. And, possibly, Jane and Cassandra with their sleeves rolled up, showing the maid servant how to make a good apple pie—'so important to their happiness!'" continued Bowden.

A popular holiday food was Yorkshire Pie, which was traditionally served on the Feast of Stephen, December 26th and afterwards. According to Wakefield, "From York-

Traditional Yorkshire Christmas Pie

shire originally, where there was a thriving trade at Christmas sending the pies around the country as gifts in the festive season, they were great pies filled with many different kinds of meat, intended to feed many people over many days. The concept was to cut off the crust lid, chop up the cooked meat within, serve everyone . . . some of each of the different the meats, then recover the remaining meat with clarified butter and re-seal the crust lid, to serve more people another day."

Yorkshire Christmas Pie
from The English Art of Cookery *by Richard Briggs*

Take a fine large turkey, a good, large fowl, a par-
tridge, a pigeon, and bone them all nicely; beat half an
ounce of mace, half an ounce of nutmegs, a quarter
of an ounce of cloves, half an ounce of white pepper
ground, and two large spoonfuls of salt, all mixed to-
gether, open all the fowls down the back, lay the tur-

key on the dresser, season it on the inside, lay the good breast downwards in the turkey, then season the goose, put in the fowl the same way, then the partridge, then the pigeon, close them together, to make them look like a whole turkey, as well as you can; case and bone a hare, and cut it into pieces, with six woodcocks, moor game, or small wild fowl, all boned; make a bushel of flour with ten pounds of butter into a paste, as directed, make the bottom and sides very thick, and raise it as high as you can, put in some seasoning, then lay the turkey, and company breasts uppermost, lay the hare on one side, and the woodcocks, moor game, or small wild fowl, on the other side, sprinkle seasoning over all, put four pounds of butter on the top, lay on a thick lid, ornament the sides and top, but first rub it over with the yolk of an egg, put paper over it, and bake in a hot oven for six hours; let it stand until it is cold before you cut it. It will keep a good while.

To finish the meal properly, Jane and Cassandra would have made a mince pie. Especially popular in Britain, this sweet, fruit-based mincemeat pie was traditionally served during the holiday season and was often referred to as a Christmas pie. Amazingly, this food dates back to the time of the Crusades of the 13th century when European crusaders brought with them Middle Eastern recipes containing meats, fruits, and spices. More than likely, the ingredients were a mixture of minced meat, suet, a range of fruits, and spices such as cinnamon, cloves, and nutmeg.

We know Jane had a fondness for these, as did most people of the day. Austen wrote in *Persuassion* of the variety of pies loaded on Mrs. Musgrove's festive trestle tables at Uppercross:

On one side was a table occupied by some chattering girls, cutting up silk and gold paper; and on the other were tressels and trays, bending under the weight of brawn and cold pies, where riotous boys were holding high revel; the whole completed by a roaring Christmas fire, which seemed determined to be heard in spite of all the noise of the others.

Jane and Cassandra might have begun to prepare the fruit and spice filling months before it was required for cooking. It would be stored in jars where the mixture would begin to macerate. As Britain entered the Victorian age, the addition of meat had gone by the by, though the use of suet remained.

There was some religious association with Christmas pies. Though the Puritans frowned on them (what didn't they frown on?), the list of thirteen ingredients were at one time thought to be representative of Christ and his twelve Apostles (according to author Margaret Baker). By Dickens' time, this religious attachment had been fairly forgotten.

The tradition of eating Christmas pie in December continued through to the Victorian era. By the time Dickens popularized mince pies, they had become much sweeter and came in a smaller, oblong shape.

Mince Pies Without Meat
from The New London Family Cook
by Duncan MacDonald

Six pounds of apples, pared, cored, and minced; of fresh suet, and raisins stoned, three pounds each: to these add of mace and cinnamon a quarter of an ounce each. And eight cloves powdered, three pounds of powdered sugar, three quarters of an ounce of salt, the rinds of four and juice of two lemons, half a pint of port, and the same of brandy. Mix well, and put into a deep pan. Have already washed and dried four pounds of currants, and, as you make the pies, add candied fruit.

Lemon Mince Pie

Squeeze a lemon, boil the outside till tender, enough to beat to a mash, add it to three apples chopped, four ounces of suet, half a pound of currants, four ounces of sugar; put the juice of the lemon and candied fruit, as for other pies. Make a short crust, and fill the patty-pans.

Trifle may have also been on the table during the Christmastide season. Trifle is an English dessert dish with layers of thick custard, fruit, sponge cake (often soaked in sherry or other fortified wine), fruit juice or jelly (gelatin in American English), and whipped cream. The earliest use of the name 'trifle' was for a thick cream flavored with sugar, ginger, and rosewater, the recipe for which was published in England, 1596, in a book called *The Good Huswife's Jewell* by Thomas Dawson. Eggs, custards, and soaked breads were thought to be added a generation or two afterwards.

Here are two trifle recipes of the period, one from Martha's own collection, and one from an 18th-century cookbook. "As you can tell, these recipes call for an extraordinary amount of alcohol. Perhaps this was to counteract the lack of refrigeration," wrote Boyle.

A *Trifle from* Martha Lloyd's Household Book

Take three Naple biscuits. Cut them in slices. Dip them in sack. Lay them on the bottom of your dish. Then make a custard of a pint of cream and five eggs and put over them. Them make a whipt syllabub as light as possible to cover the whole. The higher it is piled, the handsomer it looks.

A *Whipt Syllabub*
from Ed. Kidder's Cookbook 1720-1740

Take a pt of cream with a spoonfull of orange flower water 2 or 3 ounces of fine sugar ye juice of a lemon ye white of 3 eggs wisk these up together & having in your glasses rhennish wine & sugar & clarret & sugar lay on ye broth with a spoon heapt up as leight as you can.

On the tables at Chawton Cottage one might have also found jellies, which were very popular at that time.

Covering the varieties of jellies in the Georgian period, J. F. Wakefield wrote that there was a "plethora of recipes from the era for such wonderful and now sadly forgotten confections such as playing card jellies, a nest of eggs jelly, moon and stars in jelly, and Oranges en Rubans or Jellies a la Bellevue. These are, in fact, small clementines or tangerine skins filled alternately with red wine jelly and white flummery . . . "

Jane was no stranger to jellies, and mentioned them in her novel *Mansfield Park*:

It was a heavy, melancholy day. Soon after the second breakfast, Edmund bade them good–bye for a week, and mounted his horse for Peterborough, and then all were gone. Nothing remained of last night but remembrances, which she had nobody to share in. She talked to her aunt Bertram— she must talk to somebody of the ball; but her aunt had seen so little of what had passed, and had so little curiosity, that it was heavy work. Lady Bertram was not certain of anybody's dress or anybody's place at supper but her own. "She could not recollect what it was that she had heard about one of the Miss Maddoxes, or what it was that Lady Prescott had noticed in Fanny: she was not sure whether Colonel Harrison had been talking of Mr. Crawford or of William when he said he was the finest young man in the room— somebody had whispered something to her; she had forgot to ask Sir Thomas what it could be." And these were her longest *speeches and clearest communications: the rest was only a languid "Yes, yes; very well; did you? did he? I did not see that; I should not know one from the other." This was very bad. It was only better than Mrs. Norris's sharp answers would have been; but she being gone home with all the supernumerary jellies to nurse a sick maid, there was peace and good-humour in their little party, though it could not boast much beside.*

The Christmastide of 1809 was a quiet one, but immensely important. Ensconced in a stable and quiet environment, the familiar patterns of country life provided Jane Austen with the time and inclination to renew her writing, which she had largely abandoned during her time in Bath. And this new life at Chawton Cottage gave her the time to do it, which was equally important.

"Jane was allowed private time. Having no room of her own [she and Cassandra shared a room], she established herself near the little-used front door, and here 'she wrote upon small sheets of paper which could easily be put away, or covered with a piece of blotting paper.' A creaking swing door gave her warning when anyone was coming, and she refused to have the creak remedied," wrote Tomalin in *The Guardian*.

Jane's writing table from this period is still at Chawton Cottage. "[It] has an octagonal table top on a baluster and acorn turned column and scroll tripod supports. The table was bought from a grandson of James Goodchild, who lived in Chawton village in Jane Austen's time. His brother-in-law, Mr Littleworth, was employed by Mrs. George Austen, Jane's mother, and when he was too old to work she furnished a cottage for him. Among the furniture was this table."

According to the Heritage 100, an Arts Council England organization, the "little table is perhaps the most iconic item associated with Jane Austen and her writing, because it was here that Jane Austen wrote her novels. Many people are moved to tears when they see it, realizing the great works of genius which were produced at it. She wrote on very small pieces of paper and compared her work to that of a miniaturist—'the two inches of ivory on which I write with so fine a brush.' Jane Austen used a quill pen to write her novels at this table."

"The liberating circumstances at Chawton, and the end of any marriage plan she might have been harboring, freed her to

Ink well & quill

concentrate on her work. This is precisely what she did at Chawton during the years 1809 and 1810," wrote biographer John Halperin. "More and more, as the years went by, she devoted herself to her work. She found she could write comfortably and securely at Chawton; she felt she belonged there, that she would not soon be leaving."

"The consensus among Jane Austen's nieces and nephews seem to be that though in her mid-thirties (the novelist turned thirty-four in December 1809), she had not lost any of her youthful charm or her slim figure or her bight eyes— or the impression she gave of 'health and animation,'" continued Halperin. "She deliberately dressed herself, as did Cassandra, in the style of older women who no longer went in for fashion or [were] interested in keeping up with it . . . It must be said in Jane's defense that there were no theaters or assembly rooms near Chawton—nothing much to dress up for."

"Jane spent the first eighteen months at Chawton preparing *Sense and Sensibility* and *First Impressions* for publication," wrote Jon Spence. "Jane's only consistent habit of revision seems to have been her need to make her work contemporary—up to date. She intended to give picture of the world her readers inhabited more or less at the moment of their reading."

It was at this table she revised the manuscripts of *Sense and Sensibility* (published in 1811) and *Pride and Prejudice* (published in 1813), both of which went to London to be published. While at this table, she created *Mansfield Park*, *Emma* and *Persuasion*.

1815

PART SIX: 1815

The year 1815 has an enormous historical significance, which of course includes the publishing of *Emma* during the Christmastide season. But more importantly, it was the year of the great Battle of Waterloo. Certainly, in Jane's personal life, Trafalgar might have occupied a more conspicuous place, since she had brothers in the British Navy, but the Battle of Waterloo on June 18, 1815 was of huge importance to Britain on many levels. And it greatly affected the fortunes of her family.

Much of it had to do with her favorite brother, Henry. But from here, a little backstory is important.

"1813 brought both good fortune and tragic loss. Uncle Leigh Perrot and his brother, Edward (Austen) Knight, helped to secure Henry's appointment as Receiver-General for Oxfordshire. His happiness was marred, however, by Eliza's death after a painfully debilitating illness. Henry soon moved to quarters over the bank at 10 Henrietta Street and, later, back to Chelsea, 23 Hans Place," wrote Austen authority J. David Grey. "Jane was entertained at both establishments. In 1815, on her visit to Hans Place during negotiations for new editions of her first three novels and the publication of *Emma*, Henry became seriously ill. Fortunately, he recovered . . . "

"For most of Jane Austen's life, England was a country at war. Yet, famously, her novels rarely hint at this fact. Her characters may include several handsome officers, but they appear less as fighting men than as gentlemen in uniform whose principal maneuvers concern the capture of female hearts, not the storming of French garrisons," wrote biographer David Nokes. "Absence of war is a condition of Jane Austen's fiction much prized by modern readers, who find great charm in her apparent depiction of a tranquil realm of domestic harmony and rural peace. The temptation to view Jane Austen's chosen fictional milieu ('3 or 4 families in a country village') as an accurate social microcosm of Regency England has proved irresistibly beguiling to readers wishing to discover, in the pages of her novels, a lost England of

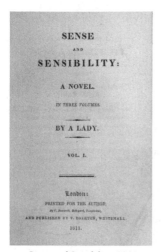

Sense and Sensibility, 1811

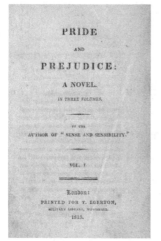

Pride and Prejudice, 1813

innocent pride and family comic prejudices," added Nokes.

By this time, Jane had become a celebrated author. The publication of *Sense and Sensibility* and *Pride and Prejudice* had made her very popular, and she had money to show for it for the first time in her life.

"The unmarried daughter of a vicar, without money or connections, she had become linked to another world where rewards of all kinds were promised," wrote novelist Carol Shields.

Now Jane was at work on her next book, *Emma*. She had begun writing the book in January 1814, and finished it in March 1815.

"After Waterloo (1815) England's economy was depressed and Henry's bank was forced into bankruptcy. Henry's last task before leaving London was to buy back the manuscript of *Catherine* (*Northanger Abbey*) from the publisher, Crosby, to whom he had sold it in 1803. Crosby obviously did not realize that the anonymous 'Lady' author was the woman who had written *Pride and Prejudice*," wrote Grey.

Austen had already made more than six hundred pounds from her first two novels, and the advance for her third. "She certainly knew *Lady Susan* was worth a lot more than 10 pounds," wrote Jon Spence. "[U]sing Henry as intermediary, she bought back the manuscript."

Her publisher "Murray, who had spotted a winner, offered 450 pounds for *Emma* but wanted the copyrights of *Mansfield Park* and *Sense and Sensibility* included. Jane was angry and told Cassandra wearily that he was a rogue, and she was likely to publish *Emma* herself," wrote Valerie Grosvenor Myer.

"From September till the end of the year, Jane spent much of her time in London, at Han Place, waiting for Murray to make up his mind about *Emma*. For all his charm, she soon found the man to be almost as mercenary a scoundrel as the others in his trade," wrote Nokes.

"Eventually a deal was struck: Murray would publish 2,000 copies of *Emma* on commission and would print a second edition of *Mansfield Park* with a print run of 750, also on commission," concluded Myer.

That autumn Henry was very seriously ill. He had seen physicians and apothecaries, and suffered huge bloodlettings. All the while Jane was editing the pages of *Emma*.

"Printing began while Henry's illness grew worse. The doctors were so alarmed that Jane sent urgently for James and Edward," wrote Claire Tomalin. Fortunately, the crisis passed. Henry was still seriously ill, but certainly more stable.

Near the end of November, 1815, Jane wrote to Cassandra of London and Henry:

> *He was out yesterday; it was a fine sunshiny day here (in the country perhaps you might have clouds and fogs. Dare I say so? I shall not deceive you, if I do, as to my estimation of the climate of London), and he ventured first on the balcony and then as far as the greenhouse. He caught no cold, and therefore has done more to-day, with great delight and self-persuasion of improvement.*

"One day a second and grander doctor who had been called in, Dr. Matthew Baillie, who had treated Henry earlier for chest trouble, mentioned to Jane that the Prince, later to become King George IV, was a great admirer of [her] novels, adding that he read them often, and even kept a set in each of his residences. The Prince, though dissolute in his private life, was a man of taste and culture with an interest in languages, history, art and literature," wrote Myer.

"The result was that the Prince's librarian, James Stanier Clarke, was told to call on her and invite her to visit the library at Carlton House. This she did, on November 13th. She remained entirely silent on the subject of its splendors and equally so on her feelings about the visit," wrote Tomalin.

"Jane Austen found herself being taken on a personally conducted tour round the royal residence of Carlton House. She is likely to have Mr. Clarke as a character to please anyone who loved to laugh: obsequious, pretentious, inept, with a Collins-like reverence for the nobility and without a ray of humor," opined David Cecil, a former Jane Austen Society president.

"Mr. Clarke was also deputed to convey to her that she might dedicate her next book to the Prince Regent," wrote Tomalin.

Jane did not approve of the Prince Regent. He had a flair for extravagance, dressed riotously, kept company with the famed Beau Brummel, and counted a court of ne'er-do-well, but well-dressed gentlemen. He spent massive sums of money. His lifestyle, and he in particular, were constantly lampooned in the press, where he was drawn to be obese and suffering from gout all the while debauching himself with food, drink, and lewd women. The Prince at one point paid off several cartoonists by buying up their sheets in order to keep them from being circulated publicly. On the other hand, he was a driving part of the new Regency style, which epitomized Britain at the time, as a real successor or conqueror of Napoleon. It is the Prince who gave us the Regency, and set the tone of style in England for a generation or more. The elegant settings of Jane's novels, and the airs of her characters, come from an era heavily influenced by this grotesque and debauched figure.

More important to Jane was his relationship with the queen. The Prince of Wales, who later became the Prince Regent, and later king, and his wife, Caroline of Brunswick-Wolfenbüttel (the Princess of Wales), had become estranged within a few years after their marriage in 1795. Caroline seemed to win much favor in the court of public opinion, despite her own shortcomings and indiscretions. The Prince Regent was successful in excluding her from official privileges, though never fully divorcing her.

In a letter to Martha Lloyd, on February 16th, 1813, Jane opined, "I suppose all the World is sitting in Judgement upon the Princess of Wales's Letter. Poor woman, I shall support her as long as I can, because she is a Woman, & because I hate her Husband—but I can hardly forgive her for calling herself 'attached & affectionate' to a Man whom she must detest—& the intimacy said to subsist between her & Lady Oxford is bad—I do not know what to do about it; but if I must give up the Princess, I am resolved at least always to think that she would have been respectable, if the Prince had behaved only tolerably by her at first."

On Sunday, November 26th, Jane wrote from Hans Place to Cassandra at Chawton:

I did mention the P. R. in my note to Mr. Murray; it brought me a fine compliment in return. Whether it has done any other good I do not know, but Henry thought it worth trying.

I hope you have told Martha of my first resolution of letting nobody know that I might dedicate, etc., for fear of being obliged to do it, and that she is thoroughly convinced of my being influenced now by nothing but the most mercenary motives. I have paid nine shillings on her account to Miss Palmer; there was no more owing.

"Jane Austen was obviously exasperated by this high-handed treatment; she was invited to look over the library at Carlton House, but never introduced to the Regent; and the pompous letters from the librarian irritated her. Thus, although she saw the unwisdom of rejecting the Prince's offer, she got her own back by mimicking the librarian's writing style" wrote Ester Davies and Gwynneth Ashby of *Literary Detectives*.

> TO HIS ROYAL HIGHNESS THE PRINCE REGENT,
>
> THIS WORK IS,
>
> BY HIS ROYAL HIGHNESS'S PERMISSION,
>
> MOST RESPECTFULLY DEDICATED,
>
> BY HIS ROYAL HIGHNESS'S DUTIFUL AND OBEDIENT
>
> HUMBLE SERVANT,
>
> THE AUTHOR

This was not the original dedication Jane wrote. She was vexed, and originally added a very simple dedication to *Emma*: "Dedicated by Permission to HRH The Prince Regent."

"[Until] John Murray put her right," wrote Tomalin. Murray insisted on something more flowery. "Martha Lloyd teased Jane about her mercenary motives in making the dedication; in fact she had resisted the idea until it was pointed out that a royal suggestion was a royal command. Murray was happy, of course . . ."

"Furthermore, Colleen A. Sheehan points out that 'In an 1814 scathing, personal letter to [the Prince Regent], which was afterwards made public, Princess Caroline repeatedly addressed her husband as 'His Royal Highness,' and she suggests that the frequent repetition of these words in the dedication refers to this letter," wrote Davies and Ashby. "There are also echoes in this adult dedication of Jane Austen's juvenilia, which are often 'Dedicated by permission' by 'Your most obedient and humble servant.' Thus, Jane Austen makes very clear that she certainly had no more respect for the Regent than she did for her own family,"

It was clear that Austen was not at all happy with the dedication. And there is a question as to whether she was so clever, or whether John Murray slipped in the three His Royal Highnesses.

The Prince Regent received his specially bound copy of *Emma* in London, in December 1815. The prince's librarian eventually wrote to her in the spring of 1816 from Brighton, "I have to return to you the Thanks of His Royal Highness the Prince Regent for the handsome Copy you sent him of your last excellent Novel . . . Lord St. Helens and many of the nobility who have been staying here, paid you the just tribute of their praise."

Yet, there was no opinion of the Prince Regent himself, nor was there any confirmation that he had in fact read it. Jane wrote to Murray later on, "Whatever he may think of my share of the work, Yours seems to have been quite right."

"[Murray's] sales plans for her *Emma* began while she was in town—and she was hopeful for this new child. It was announced in the Morning Post on December 2nd and 6th, 1815, and on Sunday, December 10th, the observer frankly promised it 'on Saturday next.' Seeing that advertisement, Jane settled a few last points with Murray and warned she would be at Hans Place till the 16th, but after that, at Chawton. When would her novel appear? The 16th passed with nothing to show," wrote Park Honan.

"Mr. Clarke must have found Jane Austen a sympathetic personality, for he now proceeded to pursue his acquaintance with her," wrote Georgian historian David Cecil.

Though she thought Mr. Clarke ridiculous, he did offer her several lines she eventually took to heart and fleshed out rather well, but did nothing with. Also, he understood her dilemma, being trapped in London by family connections and the publication of her book.

"Pray, dear Madam, remember, that besides My Cell at Carlton House, I have another which Dr. Barne procured for me at No: 37 Golden Square—where I often hide myself. There is a small Library there much at your service—and if you can make the Cell render you any service as a sort of Half-way house, when you come to town—I shall be most happy."

Still, Jane was never idle very long during her stay in London. She wrote constantly of Henry, his health and her own society while there.

Well, we were very busy all yesterday; from half-past eleven till four in the streets, working almost entirely for other people, driving from place to place after a parcel for Sandling, which we could never find, and encountering the miseries of Grafton House to get a purple frock for Eleanor Bridges. We got to Keppel St., however, which was all I cared for; and though we could stay only a quarter of an hour, Fanny's calling gave great pleasure, and her sensibility still greater, for she was very much affected at the sight of the children. Poor little F. looked heavy. We saw the whole party.

Aunt Harriet hopes Cassy will not forget to make a pincushion for Mrs. Kelly, as she has spoken of its being promised her several times. I hope we shall see Aunt H. and the dear little girls here on Thursday.

So much for the morning. Then came the dinner and Mr. Haden, who brought good manners and clever conversation. From seven to eight the harp; at eight Mrs. L. and Miss E. arrived, and for the rest of the evening the drawing-room was thus arranged: on the sofa

*side the two ladies, Henry, and myself making the best
of it; on the opposite side Fanny and Mr. Haden, in two
chairs (I believe, at least, they had two chairs), talking
together uninterruptedly. Fancy the scene! And what is
to be fancied next? Why, that Mr. H. dines here again
to-morrow. To-day we are to have Mr. Barlow. Mr.
H. is reading "Mansfield Park" for the first time, and
prefers it to P. and P.*

*A hare and four rabbits from Gm. yesterday, so
that we are stocked for nearly a week.*

Jane wrote again in early December to Cassandra:

*Mr. Meyers gives his three lessons a week, altering
his days and his hours, however, just as he chooses,
never very punctual, and never giving good measure. I
have not Fanny's fondness for masters, and Mr. Meyers does not give me any longing after them. The truth
is, I think, that they are all, at least music-masters,
made of too much consequence, and allowed to take
too many liberties with their scholars' time.*

*We shall be delighted to see Edward on Monday,
only sorry that you must be losing him. A turkey will
be equally welcome with himself. He must prepare*

for his own proper bedchamber here, as Henry moved down to the one below last week; he found the other cold.

I am sorry my mother has been suffering, and am afraid this exquisite weather is too good to agree with her. I enjoy it all over me, from top to toe, from right to left, longitudinally, perpendicularly, diagonally; and I cannot but selfishly hope we are to have it last till Christmas—nice, unwholesome, unseasonable, relaxing, close, muggy weather.

On her birthday, December 16th, 1815, there appeared in a newspaper an advertisement promoting her book. But the book itself had yet to materialize. Jane could not account for the delay and was very frustrated. Disappointed, Jane collected her things, and spent her birthday in a carriage, on her way back to Chawton, so that she would return home for the remainder of the Christmastide season.

"[*Emma*] was announced in the *Morning Chronicle* for December 21st, 22nd, and 23rd, 1815, as '*by the Author of Pride and Prejudice*'; it was also mentioned in the observer for December 10th as forthcoming. *Emma* did indeed appear in December, 1815, though its title page is dated 1816," wrote Halperin.

On December 23rd, 1815 an advertisement for Murray's Publishing announced Jane's book 'Published This Day' in time for Christmas: *Emma*.

"As in the case of *Mansfield Park*, she collected her friends' opinions of *Emma*, but this new work was reviewed favorably if perfunctorily in the *Literary Panorama*, *The Monthly Review*, *The British Critic*, and *The Gentleman's Magazine*. More important, was the extended criticism in the issue dated October, 1815, but which did not appear until March, 1816 of John Murray's influential *Quarterly Review*," wrote biographer Joan Rees.

"That Christmas, Jane busied herself dispatching presentation sets of *Emma* to select friends and relations. She sent one set to the Countess of Morley, a new friend, to whom she had been introduced by Henry earlier that year. Lady Morely had once been rumored to be the true authoress of *Pride and Prejudice*, but Jane did not begrudge her this moment of borrowed fame. It was something of a compliment, she thought," wrote Nokes. Lady Morely praised the book.

"Although unsigned, the well-considered and highly favorable review of more than four thousand words produced by the popular and successful Walter Scott, whose style many would probably recognize, was an important step forward in the founding of her reputation," reasoned Rees.

Many years later, Scott gained an even deeper appreciation for Austen's work. On March 14th, 1826, he wrote in his journal about Austen, "That young lady had a talent for describing the involvement and feelings and characters of ordinary life which is to me the most wonderful I ever met with. The Big Bow-Wow strain I can do myself like any now going, but the exquisite touch which renders the ordinary commonplace things and characters interesting from the truth of the description and the sentiment is denied to me."

Emma had found a home with the public, and the rights to the unpublished novel *Susan* would soon be restored to Jane. Despite the disappointment of leaving London without the physical book in her hand, it was as good a Christmas season as Jane could have hoped for in a literary career.

"*Say 'No' if it is to be said.*"   *She could really say nothing*

Illustration of Mr Knightley and Emma Woodhouse by Chris Hammond

Two
Christmases

EPILOGUE

Jane was slowly but unmistakably slowing down. First perceived by her as a sign of aging, it was clear with each day that she was becoming perceptibly weaker and more tired. Soon it was apparent that it was not the normal process of slowing down, but of something more deadly. What doctors could not have known then is that Jane was most likely suffering from Addison's disease. At the time, there were no known treatments for this disease.

"For the first time, it [was] plain that Jane's health had been giving rise to serious concern," wrote Joan Rees.

"Late in 1816, her fickle illness tired her. Since her mother preferred the only downstairs sofa, Jane rested on three hard chairs. 'I think she had a pillow, but it never looked comfortable.' Wrote Caroline, who heard she avoided the sofa for fear her mother would not use it," wrote Honan. "She walked slowly, but treated her debility lightly and (to amuse a niece) called herself, 'J.A.', the old Jackass. 'Not so stout as the old Jackass,' she wrote . . . "

"As news of her illness spread among her friends and relatives, she used her wit as a defense against pity she did not want, and against humiliation worse for her perhaps than diarrhea and pain. She was now under siege," wrote Park Honan.

By September 1816, the illness was taking its toll, and while she put a good face on many times, with Cassandra she was less stoic. "Jane admitted that her back pains were les severe, but that the cottage was wearisomely hectic," wrote Honan.

"Thank you, my back has scarcely given me any pain for many days. I have an idea that agitation does it as much harm as fatigue, and that I was ill at the time of your going from the very circumstance of your going," Jane wrote. "I wanted a few days quiet, & exemption from the thought & contrivances which any sort of company gives. Composition to me seems impossible." By this time she was eating large amounts of mutton and receiving large doses of rhubarb.

"She meant to write until she died. But with backaches, nausea and many days when she could do nothing, she needed help beyond Martha's or her sister's powers," wrote Honan.

"On what was to be her last birthday, Jane wrote to Edward. He was a lucky nephew to receive such a wise and humorous letter," wrote Rees. In the letter, Austen congratulated her nephew on graduating from Winchester. All good-natured fun, she wrote.

Chawton, Monday, Dec. 16th, 1816

My Dear E.,

One reason for my writing to you now is, that I may have the pleasure of directing to you Esqre. I give you joy of having left Winchester. Now you may own how miserable you were there; now it will gradually all come out, your crimes and your miseries—how often you went up by the Mail to London and threw away fifty guineas at a tavern, and how often you were on the point of hanging yourself, restrained only, as some ill-natured aspersion upon poor old Winton has it, by the want of a tree within some miles of the city. Charles Knight and his companions passed through Chawton about 9 this morning; later than it used to be. Uncle Henry and I had a glimpse of his handsome face, looking all health and good humour. I wonder when you will come and see us. I know what I rather speculate upon, but shall say nothing. We think uncle Henry in excellent looks. Look at him this moment, and think so too, if you have not done it before; and we have the great comfort of seeing decided improvement in uncle Charles, both as to health, spirits, and appearance. And they are each of them so agreeable in their different way, and harmonise so well, that their visit is thorough enjoyment. Uncle Henry writes very superior sermons. You and I must try to get hold of one or two, and put them into our novels: it would be a fine help to a volume; and we could make our heroine read it aloud on a Sunday evening, just as well as Isabella Wardour, in the "Antiquary," is made to read the "History of the Hartz Demon" in the ruins of St. Ruth, though I believe, on recollection, Lovell is the reader. By the bye, my dear E., I am quite concerned for the loss your mother mentions in her letter. Two chapters and a half to be missing is monstrous! It is well that I have not been at Steventon lately, and therefore cannot be suspected of purloining them: two strong twigs and a half towards a nest of my own would have been something. I do not think, however, that any theft of that sort would be really very useful to me. What should I do with your strong, manly, vigorous sketches, *full of variety and glow? How could I possibly join them on to the little bit (two inches wide) of ivory on which I work with so fine a brush, as produces little effect after much labour?*

'You will hear from uncle Henry how well Anna is. She seems perfectly recovered. Ben was here on Saturday, to ask uncle Charles and me to dine with them, as to-morrow, but I was forced to decline it, the walk is beyond my strength (though I am otherwise very well), and this is not a season for donkey-carriages; and as we do not like to spare uncle Charles, he has declined it too.

Tuesday. Ah, ah! Mr. E. I doubt your seeing uncle Henry at Steventon to-day. The weather will prevent your expecting him, I think. Tell your father, with aunt Cass's love and mine, that the pickled cucumbers are extremely good, and tell him also—"tell him what you will." No, don't tell him what you will, but tell him that grandmamma begs him to make Joseph Hall pay his rent, if he can.

'You must not be tired of reading the word uncle, for I have not done with it. Uncle Charles thanks your mother for her letter; it was a great pleasure to him to know that the parcel was received and gave so much satisfaction, and he begs her to be so good as to give three

shillings for him to Dame Staples, which shall be allowed
for in the payment of her debt here.

Adieu, Amiable! I hope Caroline behaves well to you.

Yours affecly,
J. Austen

At the turn of the year there was a seasonal letter to
Anna, thanking her for a turkey, and good will wishes to
Cassy on the New Year of 1817, which she wrote all the
words backwards.

At one point, she wrote to Alethea near the end of
January:

Chawton, January 24th, 1817

My Dear Alethea,

I think it time there should be a little writing between us,
though I believe the epistolary debt is on your side, and
I hope this will find all the Streatham party well, neither
carried away by the flood, nor rheumatic through the
damps. Such mild weather is, you know, delightful to us,
and though we have a great many ponds, and a fine run-

ning stream through the meadows on the other side of the road, it is nothing but what beautifies us and does to talk of. I have certainly gained strength through the winter and am not far from being well; and I think I understand my own case now so much better than I did, as to be able by care to keep off any serious return of illness. I am convinced that bile is at the bottom of all I have suffered, which makes it easy to know how to treat myself. You will be glad to hear thus much of me, I am sure. We have just had a few days' visit from Edward, who brought us a good account of his father, and the very circumstance of his coming at all, of his father's being able to spare him, is itself a good account. He grows still, and still improves in appearance, at least in the estimation of his aunts, who love him better and better, as they see the sweet temper and warm affections of the boy confirmed in the young man: I tried hard to persuade him that he must have some message for William but in vain . . . This is not a time of year for donkey-carriages, and our donkeys are necessarily having so long a run of luxurious idleness that I suppose we shall find they have forgotten much of their education when we use them again. We do not use two at once however; don't imagine such excesses . . . Our own new clergyman is expected here very soon, perhaps in time to assist Mr. Papillon on Sunday. I shall be very glad when the first hearing is over. It will be a nervous hour for our pew, though we hear that he acquits himself with as much ease and collectedness, as if he had been used to it all his life. We have no chance we know of seeing you between Streatham and Winchester: you go the other road and are engaged to two or three houses; if there should be any change, however, you know how welcome you would be . . . We have been reading the "Poet's Pilgrimage to Waterloo," and generally with much approbation. Nothing will please all the world, you know; but parts of it suit me better than much that he has written before. The opening--the proem I believe he calls it--is very beautiful. Poor man! one cannot but grieve for the loss of the son so fondly described. Has he at all recovered it? What do Mr. and Mrs. Hill know about his present state?

Yours affly,
J. Austen

The real object of this letter is to ask you for a recipe, but I thought it genteel not to let it appear early. We remember some excellent orange wine at Manydown, made from Seville oranges, entirely or chiefly. I should *be very much obliged to you for the recipe, if you can command it within a few weeks.'*

Jane's spirits were evidently high enough to harass, however gently, another for an orange wine recipe. She had written to her niece Caroline on January 23rd, 1817, consulting her niece's attempts at writing, and humorously writes later, "The Piano Forte often talks of you; — in various keys, tunes & expressions I allow — but be it Lesson or Country dance, Sonata or Waltz, You are really its constant Theme." Jane also wrote, "I feel myself getting stronger than I was half a year ago, & can so perfectly well walk to Alton, or back again, without the slightest fatigue that I hope to be able to do both when summer comes."

By April 27th she had penned her final will, and on July 18th, 1817 she was gone. Jane passed in the arms of her sister, Cassandra. She was interred at her brother Henry's direction in an aisle of the nave of Winchester Cathedral. She was forty-one years old.

That December, 1817, *Northanger Abbey and Persuasion* are both published. Again, the title page was always a year out, citing 1818.

"*Persuasion* and *Northanger Abbey* were published together by Miss Austen's brother, Henry Austen," wrote Austen scholar Ann Haker. "While she had published anonymously during her lifetime, Henry was always eager to let everyone know of the talents of his beloved sister. In publishing these last two of her novels, Henry wished the world to know the identity of the author of *Pride and Prejudice*, *Sense and Sensibility*, *Mansfield Park*, and *Emma*. He therefore wrote an introduction to the novels, telling of her authorship, her life, and her too-early death. The "Biographical Notice of the Author" is a touching memorial to the love of a brother for his sister and shows the respect and regard that he held for her."

In her own copy of *Persuasion*, Cassandra marked a passage:

How eloquent could Anne Elliott have been—how eloquent, at least were her wishes on the side of an early attachment, and a cheerful confidence in futurity, against that over anxious caution which seems to insult exertion and distrust Providence!—She had been forced into imprudence in her youth, she learned romance as she grew older—the natural sequel of an unnatural human being.

In the margins of the book, Cassandra had scribbled in her own hand, "Dear, dear Jane! This deserves to be written in letters of gold."

Selected Bibliography

Ackley, David. "Homebrew Spruce Beer Recipe." ECKraus.com. www.eckraus.com/blog/homebrew-spruce-beer-recipe#sthash.4U5kG2PK.dpuf

Austen-Leigh, William and Austen-Leigh, Richard Arthur. *Jane Austen, Her Life and Letters*. New York: Barnes & Noble, 2006.

Beckford, Martin. "Christmas Ends in Confusion over When Twelfth Night Falls." *The Daily Telegraph* (London), Jan. 6, 2009.

Beverly, Jo. "Christmas in the Regency." JoBev.com. www.jobev.com/xmasarticle.html

Bloom, Harold, ed. *Jane Austen Modern Critical Views*. New York: Chelsea House, 1986.

Bowden, Jean K. "Living in Chawton Cottage." Jane Austen Society of North America. www.jasna.org/persuasions/printed/number12/bowden.htm

Boyle, Laura. "Georgian Christmas Celebrations." Jane Austen.co.uk. www.janeausten.co.uk/georgian-christmas-celebrations/#content

Boyle, Laura. "Just a Trifle." JaneAusten.co.uk. www.janeausten.co.uk/just-a-trifle/

Boyle, Laura. "Mead: Home Brewed Honey-Wine." JaneAusten.co.uk. www.janeausten.co.uk/mead-home-brewed-honey-wine

Boyle, Laura. "Oranges and Lemons." JaneAusten.co.uk. www.janeausten.co.uk/oranges-and-lemons

Boyle, Laura. "Small Beer." JaneAusten.co.uk. www.janeausten.co.uk/small-beer

Boyle, Laura. "Spruce Beer." JaneAusten.co.uk. www.janeausten.co.uk/spruce-beer

Brooks, Walter. "The Twelve Days of Isthmus…" *Cape Cod Today*, Dec. 17, 2007. www.capecodtoday.com/blogs/Blogfather/2007/12/17/8337-12-daze-Isthmus-and-Plover-Pine-Tree

Brown, Robert. "The Manor of Manydown." *Basingstoke Gazette*. Sept. 3, 2014.

Bush, Douglas. *Jane Austen (Masters of World Literature Series)*. New York: Macmillan, 1975.

Cecil, David. *A Portrait of Jane Austen*. New York: Hill and Wang, 1980.

Davies, Ester, and Ashby, Gwenyth. "Jane Austen and the Prince Regent." Literary Detectives. www.janeaustendetectives.com/blog/search/jane-austen-and-the-prince-regent

de Guardiola, Susan. "Real Regency Dancers Don't Turn Single: Ten Tips for Judging Authenticity." Capering & Kickery.com. March 12, 2008. www.kickery.com/2008/03/regency-dancers.html

Forbes, Bruce. *Christmas: A Candid History*. Huntington, Calif.: University of California Press, 2008.

Gontar, Cybele. "Empire Style, 1800–1815." *Heilburn Timeline of Art History*. www.metmuseum.org/toah/hd/empr/hd_empr.htm

Grey, J. David. "Henry Austen: Jane Austen's 'Perpetual Sunshine.'" www.jasna.org/persuasions/printed/opno1/grey.htm

Haker, Ann. "Persuasion." Austen.com. www.austen.com/persuade

Halperin, John. *The Life of Jane Austen*. Baltimore: Johns Hopkins University Press, 1984.

Hubert, Maria. *Jane Austen's Christmas*. London: Sutton Publishing, 1996.

"A Jane Austen Christmas: Vignettes of Customs and Traditions." Historic Odessa Foundation. www.historicodessa.org/gallery/jane-austen-christmas-vignettes-customs-and-traditions

"Jane Austen's Opinion on the Infidelities of the Prince and Princess of Wales." Pemberly.com. www.pemberley.com/janeinfo/jprncwal.html

"Jane Austen's Writing Table." Heritage 100, Arts Council England. www3.hants.gov.uk/heritage100/itemlist/item.htm?itemid=139

Johnson, Ben. "A Georgian Christmas." Historic UK. www.historic-uk.com/CultureUK/A-Georgian-Christmas

Kakutani, Michiko. "She Wasn't So Placid After All." *New York Times*, Nov. 25, 1997.

Laski, Marghanita. *Jane Austen*. London: Thames and Hudson, 1975.

Lauber, John. *Jane Austen*. New York: Twayne Publishers, 1993.

Le Faye, Deirdre. *Jane Austen: The World of Her Novels*. London: Frances Lincoln, 2002.

Lee, Emery. "Historical Recipe #3 Royal Punch." GeorgianJunkie.com. Sept. 15, 2011. https://georgianjunkie.wordpress.com/tag/john-nott

MacDonagh, Oliver. *Jane Austen: Real and Imagined Worlds*. New Haven: Yale University Press, 1991.

"Manydown Park, Where It All Started." BecomingJane.com. June 17, 2007. becomingjane.blogspot.com/2007/06/manydown-house-where-it-all-started.html

Mullan, John. "The Ball in the Novels of Jane Austen." British Library. www.bl.uk/
romantics-and-victorians/articles/the-ball-in-the-novels-of-jane-austen#
sthash.ZXDxoA4o.dpuf

Myer, Valerie Grosvenor. *Jane Austen, Obstinate Heart: A Biography*. New York:
Arcade Publishing, 1997.

Norman, Andrew. *Jane Austen: An Unrequited Love*. Gloucestershire: The History
Press, 2009.

Nokes, David. *Jane Austen: A Life*. New York: Farrar Straus & Giroux, 1997.

Rees, Joan. *Jane Austen: Woman and Writer*. New York: St. Martin's Press, 1976.

Reynolds, Eileen. "The Exchange: David Wondrich on Punch." *The New Yorker*.
Dec. 13, 2010.

Sanborn, Victoria. "Dancing at the Netherfield Ball: Pride and Prejudice." Jane
Austen's World. janeaustensworld.wordpress.com/2010/06/28/dancing-at-the-
netherfield-ball-pride-and-prejudice

Sanborn, Victoria. "Jane Austen's Father: Reverend George Austen." Jane Austen's
World. janeaustensworld.wordpress.com/2010/06/20/jane-austens-father-
reverend-george-austen

Sanborn, Victoria. "Jane Austen's Writing (Sloping) Desk." Jane Austen's World.
janeaustensworld.wordpress.com/2009/04/09/jane-austens-writing-or-sloping-desk

Scott, Regina. "Christmas, Regency Style." ReginaScott.com. www.reginascott.
com/christmas.htm

Shields, Carol. *Jane Austen*. New York: Viking, 2001.

Smith, Lori. *Jane Austen's Guide to Life*. Guilford, Conn.: Skirt!, 2012.

Spence, Jon. *Becoming Jane Austen*. London: Hambledon Continuum, 2003.

"Steventon, Jane Austen's Home." Hampshire County Council. www3.hants.gov.
uk/austen/deane-parsonage/steventon-village.htm

Sullivan, Margaret C. *The Jane Austen Handbook*. Philadelphia: Quirk Books, 2007.

Sutherland, Eileen. "Dining at the Great House: Food and Drink in the Time of
Jane Austen." Jane Austen Society of North America. www.jasna.org
persuasions/printed/number12/sutherland2.htm

Sutherland, Kathryn. "Jane Austen's Juvenalia." British Library. www.bl.uk
romantics-and-victorians/articles/jane-austens-juvenilia

Tomalin, Claire. *Jane Austen: A Life*. New York: Alfred A. Knopf, 1998.

Tomalin, Claire. "Writer's Rooms: Jane Austen." *The Guardian*. July 12, 2008.
"Unlocking Secrets from Jane Austen's Steventon Home." BBC News, Dec. 26, 2013. www.bbc.com/news/uk-england-hampshire-20678244

Wakefield, J.F. "A Christmas Visit to Jane Austen's House, Part 1." www.austenonly.com/2010/12/16/a-christmas-visit-to-jane-austens-house-part-1

Wakefield, J.F. "A Christmas Visit to Jane Austen's House, Part 3." www.austenonly.com/2010/12/23/a-christmas-visit-to-jane-austens-house-part-3

Wakefield, J.F. "Book Review: Jellies and their Moulds by Peter Brears." www.austenonly.com/2010/12/13/book-review-jellies-and-their-moulds-by-peter-brears

Wakefield, J. F. "Jane Austen and Christmas: Mrs Musgrove's Pies." www.austenonly.com/2009/12/16/jane-austen-and-christmas-mrs-musgroves-pies-1

Wakefield, J.F. "Jane Austen and Christmas: Parlour Games for the Season and Twelfth Night." austenonly.com/2010/01/06/jane-austen-and-christmas-parlour-games-for-the-season-and-twelfth-night

Warren, Nathan Boughton. *The Holidays: Christmas, Easter, and Whitsuntide: Their Social Festivities, Customs, and Carols*. 1868.

Welland, Freydis Jane. "The History of Jane Austen's Writing Desk." Jane Austen Society of North America. www.jasna.org/persuasions/printed/number30/welland.pdf